Revelation

Revelation

Themes in the Doctrine and Covenants

Janiece Johnson

BYU Maxwell Institute
Brigham Young University
Provo, Utah

DESERET BOOK

© 2024 by Neal A. Maxwell Institute for Religious Scholarship,
Brigham Young University. All rights reserved. This book is the
result of a joint publishing effort by the Neal A. Maxwell Institute
for Religious Scholarship and Deseret Book Company.

Permissions. No portion of this book may be reproduced by any
means or process without the formal written consent of the
publisher. Direct all permissions requests to Permissions Manager,
Neal A. Maxwell Institute for Religious Scholarship, Brigham Young
University, Provo, UT 84602 or email: **MIpermissions@byu.edu.**

The views expressed in this book are solely those of the authors
and do not necessarily represent those of the editors, The Neal
A. Maxwell Institute for Religious Scholarship, Brigham Young
University or any of its affiliates, Deseret Book, or The Church of
Jesus Christ of Latter-day Saints.

Deseret Book is a registered trademark of Deseret Book Company.
Visit us at deseretbook.com or maxwellinstitute.byu.edu.
Printed by Sheridan Books. The paper used in this publication meets
the minimum requirements of the American National Standards for
Information Sciences—Permanence of Paper for Printed Library
Materials. ANSI Z39.48-19

ISBN: 978-0-8425-0135-4

Library of Congress Control Number: 2024942351

Cover Design: Ashley Pun

Original Cover Art: Leslie Graff, lesliegraff.com

Book Design: Kachergis Book Design

Printed in the United States of America

GENERAL EDITORS
Rosalynde Frandsen Welch
Terryl Givens

SERIES EDITORS
Lori Forsyth, Matthew Godfrey,
James Goldberg, Kristine Haglund,
Robin Jensen, Elizabeth Kuehn

PRODUCTION MANAGERS
Jeremy King, Tessa Hauglid

DESERET BOOK ACQUISITION EDITOR
Janiece Johnson

SERIES AUTHORS
Mason Allred, *Seeing*
Philip Barlow, *Time*
Justin Collings, *Divine Law*
Amy Easton, *Divine Aid*
Terryl Givens, *Agency*
Amy Harris, *Redeeming the Dead*
Janiece Johnson, *Revelation*

Series Introduction

The present series, *Themes in the Doctrine and Covenants*, seeks to magnify the truth of and build faith in latter-day revelation. "Search these commandments," the Lord instructs in His preface to the Doctrine and Covenants, "for they are true and faithful" (Doctrine and Covenants 1:37). The words of the Lord and of modern prophets recorded in this book instruct, comfort, warn, and call to repentance. Most importantly, they invite readers to find life in Christ and to join with His Church. President Ezra Taft Benson said, "The Book of Mormon brings men to Christ. The Doctrine and Covenants brings men to Christ's kingdom, even The Church of Jesus Christ of Latter-day Saints."[1] These volumes respond to that invitation with the requisite offering of the disciple's "heart and a willing mind" (Doctrine and Covenants 64:34).

While other books offer doctrinal commentary or historical context for the revelations, the present series proceeds topically. Each volume explores a central theme of the Doctrine and Covenants, tracing its meaning and development across the canonical text. The series is not intended as a comprehensive survey. Instead, each volume seeks to cast new light on one of the scripture's central concerns and to make its chosen theme relevant to present-day readers. In this, the series reflects the character of the Doctrine and Covenants itself, which is neither an integrated theological treatise nor a systematic history but a work "arrange[d from] the items of the doctrine of Jesus Christ,"[2] an ever-incomplete canonization of individual revelations intended to make God's voice audible to the modern Church.

Each of the seven authors brings to the task an academic training sufficient to place the revelations in their historical, cultural, and theological settings and to probe the meaning of the sacred text. To this academic training, each author adds faith in the gospel of Jesus Christ and the pursuit of vibrant Christian discipleship in an increasingly secular age. The series thus reflects the apostolic commission given to the Maxwell Institute "to use salvational truths [in faith-oriented scholarship] whenever and wherever [it] can."[3]

Each volume, and this series, is intended to increase the reader's understanding of and faith in the doctrines of the Church of Jesus Christ of Latter-day Saints. Nevertheless, these volumes are not official publications of the Church and do not claim to speak with authority on Church doctrines. Each author brings a personal approach to his or her exploration, and the resulting volumes are provisional by design. Taken together, *Themes in the Doctrine and Covenants* models the proper multivocality of the Church's obedience to the Lord's command "to expound scriptures, and to exhort the church.... I say unto you, that this is my voice unto all" (Doctrine and Covenants 25:7, 16). The volumes demonstrate the fruits of a serious approach to scripture study and invite readers to likewise plumb the depths of modern revelation. The series' ambition is to allow the revelations to speak with new urgency to a people thirsty for the word of God, and thereby to increase the reader's conversion to Jesus Christ. "Seek me diligently and ye shall find me," the Lord promises. "Ask, and ye shall receive; knock, and it shall be opened unto you" (Doctrine and Covenants 88:63).

Editions of the Doctrine and Covenants

In 1835, Joseph Smith wrote a letter "To the Elders of the Church" in which he expounded the parable of Jesus likening "every scribe instructed concerning the kingdom of heaven" to "a householder who brings out of his treasure things new and old" (Matthew 13:51-53).[4] Joseph then, identifying himself with the scribe, named three examples of these treasures he had assisted in bringing forth: the Book of Mormon, the (new) translation of the Bible, and "the covenants given to the Latter Day Saints." The Book of Mormon had been in print for five years; the most significant portions of his "new translation" had been published in the Church newspaper, *The Evening and Morning Star* in 1832 and 1833.[5] That left the third treasure—"the covenants"—to be brought forth.

Over preceding years, angelic visitors and the voice of God had spoken to Joseph in visions, through the Urim and Thummim, and in the quiet of his mind. The summer following the 1830 organization of the Church, Joseph and John Whitmer, recognizing that the Prophet's revelatory work continued, began to "arrange and copy" those revelations Joseph had not ceased receiving from the First Vision onwards. On the first day of November 1831, a special conference of elders assembled in Hiram, Ohio, to discuss the publication of a number of those revelations to be selected and prepared. During that conference, the Lord confirmed that the assembled revelations, a "Book of my commandments," were from Him and provided a "preface" for the collection which the assembled conference sustained. The growing body of new revelations was thereby added to the Church's canon of scripture, as the Saints embraced the continuing reality of revelation to living prophets.

A little more than a year later, printing began in Independence, Missouri, at a time of growing violence. As the laborious process neared completion, a mob attacked the print shop, destroyed the equipment, scattered the type, and dispersed the printed sheets to the wind. Two young sisters, Mary and Caroline Rollins, rescued as many pages as possible. Several copies of the first 65 sections, about two-thirds of the anticipated total, were salvaged and bound as "The Book of Commandments." The few copies this heroism made available were insufficient to satisfy demand, and the available volumes were significantly incomplete.

It was two years before the Saints had the resources

to reconstitute the collection, making edits, revisions, and additions. By 1835, Joseph had added seven "lectures on theology," recently delivered to the Kirtland "School of the Elders" under his supervision. "Theology" suggests a rigorous academic exercise, but Joseph used one of its current nineteenth-century meanings of "that *revealed* science" of God.[6] Subsequently called "The Lectures on Faith," these essays "on the doctrine of the church" accounted for the first half of the volume's new title: The *Doctrine* and Covenants. "Covenants" replaced "commandments" as the second term in the title and referred to the 103 revelations.

The year 1831 had been the period of most frequent revelations, as might be expected in the first full year of the Church's organization. Thirty-four—or about one-fourth of the volume's current contents—were received that year. By 1835, when the newly titled Doctrine and Covenants was published, another 18 were included. In the year of the Prophet's death, a second edition was published in Nauvoo, adding eight new items.

The first major revision of formatting occurred in 1876. Orson Pratt created the versification, and 26 revelations were added, almost all of which had been received by Joseph Smith but were not previously canonized. Brigham Young's epistle from Winter Quarters to "the camp of Israel" was also included. From 1908, the Official Declaration announcing the end of plural marriage was included. In 1921, recognizing that the Lectures had not been received by Church vote, they were removed—though the volume's title remained.

In 1981, two revelations previously appended to the Pearl of Great Price were included in the Doctrine and Covenants: Joseph F. Smith's 1918 vision of the dead and Joseph Smith's vision of the celestial kingdom. Also transferred was Official Declaration 2, the public announcement of the 1978 revelation that "removed all restrictions with regard to race that once applied to the priesthood."[7] Not all revelations, past or present, become canonized scripture—in fact, more than 40 revelations to the Prophet have never been included.[8]

The Book of Mormon is the keystone of the faith, vividly confirming the stream of revelation that flows unimpeded from God to humankind. Still, the Book of Mormon does not lay out those doctrines most associated with the Restoration. The Doctrine and Covenants provides the inspired foundations for what we know about premortality, eternal relationships, vicarious salvation, human exaltation, tithing, the Word of Wisdom, and much else. We hope the volumes in this series enhance your appreciation for those and other "treasures" brought forth in this dispensation.

Contents

	Series Introduction	vii
	Introduction: Revelation in Abundance	1
1.	The Voice of the Lord and Joseph Smith *Section 1*	11
2.	Hearkening and Asking *Section 46*	27
3.	Scripture Abounds *Sections 20, 76, and 138*	39
4.	My Servant, Joseph Smith, Jr. *Sections 28 and 43*	57
5.	The Tyranny of a Burning Bosom *Section 9*	69
6.	Growing into the Spirit of Revelation *Sections 6 and 8*	81
7.	Cautionary Tales *Sections 50, 51, 52, 54, 58, 60, 64*	95
8.	When Silence Reigns *Sections 98, 101, and 121*	111
	Coda: My Word Shall Not Pass Away	123
	Endnotes	129
	Scripture Index	141

Introduction

Revelation in Abundance

Whoever heard of true religion without communication with God?...
The principle of present revelation ... is the very foundation of our
religion. (John Taylor[1])

When Joseph Smith wrote a statement of belief for The Church of Jesus Christ of Latter-day Saints in 1842, he laid out 13 Articles of Faith. They were short, succinct, and expansive. In contrast to the creeds that Joseph was most familiar with, like the 33 chapters of the Westminster Confession, his creed returned to an earlier Christian model of creeds. In a single sentence, his ninth article is both concise and sweeping—"We believe all that God has revealed, all that He does now reveal, and we believe that He will yet reveal many great and important things pertaining to the Kingdom of God" (Article of Faith 9). Rather than an attempt to enumerate every jot or tittle of dogmatic religion, his creed laid a foundation for a theology of what this book calls "revelatory abundance."

While the size of this little book hints that this will not be a comprehensive examination of revelation in the Restoration, it will shed light on Joseph Smith's theology of revelatory abundance. Let's start by defining our terms. I define revelation simply as divine communication. In English, from as early as the fourteenth century, revelation was defined as "the disclosure or communication of knowledge, instructions, etc., by divine or supernatural means." Both this sense of the English revelation and the older Greek *apokalypsis* (which is translated as revelation in the New Testament) include a sense of uncovering divine things. God can both uncover and conceal divine knowledge. The etymology of the word from the Latin roots points to a variety of means: revelation might be a "manifestation," it might be "revealed truth" as it is used in the Latin Vulgate, "divine disclosure" as early church father Tertullian defined it in the late second or early third century, or it could specifically be the last book of the New Testament or any "work by an author ... in which a person's divine revelations are described."[2]

The Doctrine and Covenants self-identifies as "containing revelations given to Joseph Smith, the Prophet with some additions by his successors in the presidency of the church."[3] This collection could be thought to fit into that last definitional category of a work describing revelations. Joseph Smith received revelations in a variety of ways and mediated the Lord's word to us. They were known as covenants, commandments, and revelations. In chapter 1, we will consider the wide range of the revelations included in this book of scripture—angelic messengers, divine words mediated by prophets, questions and answers, visions, and more. This collection of commandments exemplifies the range of information that can be revealed: priesthood, missions, ritual instructions, scripture, keys, holy locations, personal directions, glory, mysteries of all kinds "which are great and marvelous," and, ultimately, the Lord can reveal Himself.

A variety of means is likewise possible. Sometimes, "the voice of inspiration steals along and whispers," and the hearer has to reach to hear; other times, a theophany unfolds with "a brightness and glory [that] defy all description" so that it can't possibly be ignored.[4] Joseph's life stands as a testament to the many ways that God can communicate with us; the revelations, too, are evidence of that revelatory abundance, but not its only evidence. This collection of revelations has multiple functions. It operates as a handbook to revelation, offering multiple models as to how we might receive revelation. Scripture can initiate the reader to learn more of God's word as well as operate as a conduit to open the way for more revelation. Part of the profusion of revelation available is to teach us how we, too, can hear the voice of God in all its variety. In an abundance of ways and directions, revelation flows out from the Restoration.

If we are to define a theology of revelatory abundance, then we need to get to the theology part. Though Latter-day

Saints don't generally label our own thinking as theological, feminist theologian Rosemary Radford-Ruether argues that theology is "God-talk."[5] It isn't just for a theologian high in an ivory tower with words only accessible to a chosen few. Theology is the work of believers thinking through and negotiating our relationship with the Divine. If we believe in God, it isn't surprising if we think about what that means in our lives. Professor Francine Bennion noted, "Good theology makes sense of what is possible but also what is presently real and probable.... It is not enough that theology be either rational or faith-promoting. It must be both. It is not enough that satisfying theology be mastered by a few expert scholars, teachers, and leaders. It must be comfortably carried by ordinary people. It is not enough that theology helps me to understand God. It must also help me to understand myself and my world."[6] Or, as Professor David Holland succinctly argued when talking about his book, *A Brief Theological Introduction to the Book of Mormon: Moroni*, in the Restoration, "everyone's a theologian."[7] We can all use more talk of God as we seek to understand our relationship with God better.

Revelation is the indispensable part of the Restoration—and our understanding of it makes us different. It is central to our existence as the restored Church of Jesus Christ, and it can come to us in a multitude of different ways. Throughout his life, Joseph revealed to us that speaking is a part of who God is. God is always a God who speaks. An element of God's character is to be in active communication with His children. Throughout this book, we will consider the common themes and modes of revelation modeled in the Doctrine and Covenants and how we see those models practically enacted in the lives of the early Saints. We recognize the commonalities of mode and experience that we can share in community and the unique ways that God speaks to each of us individually. Revelatory communication in abundance.

To consider this abundance, the chapters in this book progress thematically, each one focusing on a specific section or sections of the Doctrine and Covenants. In the first chapter, "The Voice of the Lord and Joseph Smith," we will begin with the Lord's preface to the revelations, section 1. We will compare pivotal revelatory experiences of Martin Luther and Joseph Smith and consider how those experiences and their interpretation shaped their respective theologies. Through revelation, Joseph developed his own relationship with God; for us, this is foundational yet distinct from much of Christian thought around revelation. In the latter part of the chapter, we will quantitatively begin to evaluate this revelatory abundance with modes, audiences, and genres.

The second chapter, "Hearkening and Asking," focuses on section 46 to reflect on the role of agency and our opportunity to initiate a dialogic conversation and choose to listen to God's response. The third chapter reckons with scripture as a subset of revelation and as a means for further revelation. Closely considering portions of sections 20, 76, and 138, we study the series of Joseph's revelatory acts to abolish any sense of scripture as a scarce commodity. In the fourth chapter, we will consider the Lord's antidote to the calamity of apostasy: the prophetic voice, which works in conjunction with personal revelation. Though the tension between personal revelation and prophetic privilege existed from the beginning of the Church, sections 28 and 43 help us examine two early points of contention and the continuing significance of a modern-day prophet. Chapter 5, "The Tyranny of a Burning Bosom," contemplates the dangers of a single model of revelation and explores the ever-adaptable nature of God's voice to speak in a way we will understand as we appraise the limitations of section 9 as a model. "Growing into the Principle of Revelation," the sixth chapter, reflects on learning the skill of revelation and what the Lord calls "*the* spirit of revelation" in section 8.[8] Looking at a number of the early Kirtland revelations, the seventh chapter, "Cautionary Tales," acknowledges some of the many stumbling blocks and deceptions that could impede our communication with God. "When Silence Reigns," the eighth and last chapter, contemplates those times when God seems to have stopped speaking. To learn more about this dark night of the soul, we'll explore two such moments in Joseph's experience, outlined in sections 98, 101, and 121. The coda reminds us that hearing God's voice will always be a process, but God will "lead us along" and that His word is sure.

As we comb the Doctrine and Covenants to learn more about revelatory abundance, it's worthwhile to remember that it's a different genre than the rest of scripture—a collection of sometimes disparate revelations. In the Book of Mormon, the narrative is primary. Perhaps we read Nephi's lament as he grieved after the death of his father and for his own sin and we remember our own grief, our own sin, and cry out, "O wretched [wo]man that I am!" (2 Nephi 3:17). However, in the Doctrine and Covenants, the narrative recedes into the background. It requires more of us to pull out the story surrounding the revelations. Yet, personal narrative still provides essential illumination as we search for divine understanding. Perhaps we read of the Lord commanding the New York Saints to leave their homes and farms and all they know behind to "Go to the Ohio," and we consider those times when God has asked us to leave something we love behind. It doesn't matter if it's a person, a sin, or a farm—their experience can help us negotiate our own (38:32). The revelations now published in the Doctrine and Covenants work in conjunction with the stories of Joseph Smith and the Saints. Together, they narrate the Restoration—the story of a people seeking to communicate with the Divine and how they were changed by those encounters. These revelations offer us not just a single model of communication with God but suggest that revelation is as abundant, rich, and varied as are God's children.

Abundance does not mean it's easy. Joseph never found perfect revelation conveyed in words—he could neither achieve perfect grammatical expression nor a wholly transparent communication of meaning. He studied grammar as an adult and tried to improve his ability to express himself beyond his limited education; he and others edited the revelations over time to make them more accessible to larger groups of people. But no matter the eloquence of the person mediating the words, for Joseph, the words remained ill-fitting houses for the transcendent and eternal—a "little narrow prison[—]almost as it were totel darkness," as he wrote to W. W. Phelps. The perfect revelation existed somewhere outside the "crooked broken scattered and imperfect language."[9] Though a perfect language isn't accessible by mere mortals, the Spirit provides the conduit, a bridge, to the perfect revelation—perfect in metaphysical elocution and understanding. The Spirit has the possibility of expanding the reception of divine ideas beyond specific earthbound words.

Perhaps this is what Paul was suggesting as he wrote to the Corinthians, "For now we know in part and we prophesy in part. But when that which is perfect is come, then that which is in part shall be done away." Both Paul and Joseph looked forward to the time when we no longer "look through a glass darkly" (1 Corinthians 13:9–10, 12). Our mortal experience compared to that ancient mirror of polished metal reminds us that here, everything appears a little distorted. Mortality is always going to offer a limited view of "things as they really are" (Jacob 4:13), and language will never quite capture the reality of what it strains to represent. However, its limitations do not negate the possibility of abundance. For now, we can be grateful for the part we do have, which is consistently made clearer through that connection with the Spirit. (Paul would also add that charity likewise does wonders to help clear that dark glass.)

Each week, as we partake of the sacrament and return to our covenant to take Christ's name upon us, we hear the promise that if we stay in the covenant, we "may always have His spirit with" us (Moroni 4:3, Doctrine and Covenants 20:77.) Perhaps the repetition of the ritual makes it easy for us to forget the immensity of this blessing. The Lord described this gift of the Spirit to longtime Methodist minister James Covell as "a blessing so great as you never have known" (39:10). Do we recognize it for the astonishing gift that it is?

Revelation's primary concern is communication, and as relationships develop and improve, so does revelation. Joseph Smith's revelations elevated the relationships of human beings to each other and to God. As we develop our own relationship with God, we will learn to better "hear Him," as President Russell M. Nelson has consistently pled with us. He has warned us that developing our facility to recognize the Spirit is of the utmost importance: "In coming days, it will not be possible to survive spiritually without the guiding, directing, comforting, and constant influence of the Holy Ghost. My beloved brothers and sisters, I plead with you to increase your spiritual capacity to receive revelation.... Choose to do the spiritual work required to enjoy the gift of the Holy Ghost and hear the voice of the Spirit more frequently and more clearly."[10] This brief book hopes to begin to consider how the Doctrine and Covenants helps us to better recognize the Spirit and develop our relationship with God so we can hear Him in all His abundance.

1

The Voice of the Lord and Joseph Smith

Section 1

From the first verse of the published revelations, Joseph Smith mediates the voice of the Lord. And in the first section of the Doctrine and Covenants, the Lord introduces us to this practical collection of God's words as conveyed by Joseph. The continuation of God's voice from the past into the present demarcates the foundation of Joseph Smith's nascent theology of revelatory abundance. Rather than God's speech ceasing with the death of the apostles, Joseph Smith's revelations and life argue for a continuity of God's voice. God is always a God who speaks. It's part of God's character to be in active communication with His children, to be in a relationship with His children. And from that first verse of the revelations, the Lord calls upon us to listen.

This chapter considers how the Lord introduces His own voice in the revelations, highlighting section 1 of the Doctrine and Covenants. We'll also compare some early epiphanies of Martin Luther and Joseph Smith—focusing on how Joseph Smith began the process of learning to hear the Lord's voice in his own life and initiated a return to revelation in abundance. We'll briefly contrast the Latter-day Saints' understanding of revelation with other Christian traditions and quantify the kinds of revelations Joseph (and others) receive. The Lord "called upon [his] servant Joseph Smith, Jun., and spake unto him from heaven" to combat the chaos of the modern world in preparation for the last days (Doctrine and Covenants 1:17). Yet, communication with God is never just the provenance of prophets; it is available to all of us. Communication with God develops and strengthens our own personal relationship with God. Joseph became someone who walked and talked with God, but that relationship did not come in a sudden burst of light. It was built over time and through many questions.

The Lord's Preface

Section 1 is not the chronological beginning of this collection of published revelations. It was given on November 1, 1831, whereas section 2 rewinds to eight years earlier. This was the day a conference of elders decided to publish Joseph Smith's contemporary revelations for the first time. After a futile attempt by three of those in attendance to pen a preface, in between the morning and afternoon sessions, Joseph asked the Lord and "received by inspiration" what the divine voice called "my preface unto the book of my commandments" (1:6).[1]

The Lord's preface to the Doctrine and Covenants begins with a bold declaration of authorship and a specific call: "Hearken, O ye people of my church, saith the voice of him who dwells on high, and whose eyes are upon all" (1:1). Claiming God's omnipotence and omnipresence, the divine voice establishes the power to call out to all humanity. The voice exhorts those in the present who profess membership in the house of God to not just listen to God's voice but to act on what is being revealed. Repetition marks the continued reminder of the divine authorship of these revelations as well as the revelations that will follow.[2]

The starting point of the revelation likewise reveals the intended audience. The Lord pleads with the "people of my church" no matter their location—whether they be near or far—and gives them the opportunity to listen together (1:1). Moreover, those already in the house are not the only ones for whom the message is important. The audience of revelation is ever-expanding until it reaches those "from afar" and those "on the isles of the sea" (1:1). The proselytizing project was innate—God's voice positioned His servants in an essential role of amplifying God's voice so that all might have the opportunity to hear.

The preface declares the power of God's voice to reach all through the senses of sight and hearing, but also through the heart: "There is none to escape" (1:2). Though God has the power to *make* all hear, coercion is not the preferred mode of communication. "Hearken" reflects agency—individuals "apply[ing] the ear to listen."[3] It's a deliberate choice to pay attention. Repeatedly, the Lord invites us to hearken and choose to listen, "that all that will hear may hear" (1:11). Listening is a function of agency—God is willing to "make all these things known unto all," but we get to choose whether or not we want to hear the voice of the Lord (1:34). And in the Restoration, chosenness or election is dependent on whether we choose to hear the Lord's voice and if we choose to let it in: "mine elect hear my voice and harden not their hearts" (29:7).

The call to hearken will persist through the revelations more than eighty times. Again and again, the Lord calls out to us. Do we choose to hear God's voice?

Martin Luther and Joseph Smith

Christians have been discussing how best to hear God for centuries. Early in Catholic monk Martin Luther's career, he studied his scriptures in the Black Tower of the monastery at Wittenberg. A moment during this time—later known as his Tower experience—became pivotal in his understanding of God. But he did not write down the experience when it happened. Nor did he ever give it a date. The lack of a contemporary historical account caused some scholars to question whether it occurred at all.[4] Yet, when he did later write of the experience, he presented it as a crucial moment in his own life that forever shifted his understanding of God. In his earliest written accounts, he described reading the first chapter of Romans and feeling "struck [in his] conscience like lightning" as if it were "like a thunderbolt in [his] heart."[5] Perhaps Luther experienced what Latter-day Saints today might call a revelatory jolt—was that God speaking to his mind and heart? Perhaps. However, over time, his descriptions and interpretations changed. Years later, the day was still remarkable to him, but he then portrayed his insight as a rational conclusion reached after careful study and meditation. The end was the same, yet the process was different. In the later accounts, he had studied the word of God and come to a rational response. There could be a reason for the shift: In the intervening years, Luther had grown fearful of the potential chaos of individual revelation, and so he encouraged order by appealing to the Bible as the highest authority.[6]

For Luther, the radical reformer Thomas Muntzer, who claimed that "all true parsons needed revelation," exemplified the real danger of prophecy.[7] If anyone could receive their own direction from God, any sense of order would be lost. Discord would be rampant, and the church would lose any sense of authority. As Luther saw it, claims to revelation ended as did Muntzer's life—amidst chaos and violence on the battlefield, fighting an unwinnable war. Luther looked to the doctrine of *sola scriptura*, elevating infallible scripture text above all other claims to divine authority to protect God's people against chaos.

In the summer of 1832, Joseph Smith, then in his mid-twenties, sat to write his own history for the first time. In his own hand, he attempted to describe a "marvilous experience" that had happened years earlier. Like Martin Luther, he would return to this moment repeatedly, and also like Luther, it took time for him to write it down. This "testamony from on high" had occurred when Joseph was a teenager. He both saw and heard God.[8] Later accounts would more specifically detail that he saw the Father and the Son, and they spoke to him. Like Martin Luther's experience in the Black Tower, Joseph's pivotal moment was initiated by the reading of scripture—believing that he "lacked wisdom" and God would "liberally" respond if he asked (James 1:5). Yet, unlike Luther, his answer did not lose its audacity in the years that followed—if anything, it gained power as he continued to learn from his experience. Joseph believed that God would literally respond to his petition. Like Luther, Joseph did not initially set out to organize a church; it was his own personal relationship with God that motivated his seeking. Hearkening to God's call led him in a direction he did not expect.

This event that we now call "the First Vision" placed the Restoration on an experiential footing. Joseph had not learned about God in the abstract. He saw God and heard God. Though he didn't fully understand this theophany instantaneously, he knew he had seen God, and God had spoken to him. He "could not deny it" (Joseph Smith—History 1:25). He hearkened and had to respond to the divine voice.

His own practical knowledge grounded his experience with the divine and shaped his theology of revelation in which God speaks, not only as a prophetic privilege to Joseph, but to all, that *all* "might speak in the name of God

IMAGE 1. Boy in Trees (ca. 1880–1920), by George Edward Anderson. Image courtesy of L. Tom Perry Special Collections, Harold B. Lee Library, Brigham Young University.

the Lord, even the Savior of the World" (1:20). What's more, this was not the sum total of Joseph's visions, but just one of "several remarkable visions."[9] This initial vision provided a footing for his theology of revelatory abundance that would be built on by subsequent encounters—additional theophanies and the beginning of a revelatory conversation with God. Yet Joseph's experience was not just about how God acts, but who God is. As we've seen, speaking is part of God's character. To speak in the present, the voice of the Lord needed a mouthpiece, just as God did anciently. God would continue to speak to Joseph and through Joseph, and Joseph would continue to respond.

From the first sentence of the published revelations in the Doctrine and Covenants, we see that revelation is based in relationship. Joseph's revelations suggest a dialogue between God and His people where agency is paramount—Terryl Givens labeled this process "dialogic revelation."[10] God may speak, but we get to choose if we listen. And then we must choose if we wish to act upon that revelation, to find relevance and guidance in our own lives. There are many mediums that God has provided for us to hear His voice. Do we immerse ourselves in scripture—in God's word? Do we hear servants of the Lord, like Joseph, modern prophets called upon to mediate the word to us? Do we listen when God's voice comes through a medium we don't expect?

Revelation in the Larger Christian Tradition

Martin Luther's discomfort with the possibility of personal communication with God is part of a larger history. The theological category of revelation has been debated by Christians for centuries. In 1983, a Jesuit priest, Avery Dulles, attempted to systematically lay out different "models of revelation." Building off the Greek *apokalypsis*, Dulles defined revelation as "an extraordinary psychic occurrence in which hidden things are suddenly made known through mental phenomena such as vision and auditions," or seeing and hearing God. However, for Dulles, seeing and hearing God are the exceptions, not the rule. He argued, "They are hardly central to the faith of Israel as a people or the self-understanding of the early Church."[11] Though Dulles did not consider all of his categories of equal importance, he offered five classic Christian models of revelation:

> DOCTRINAL: "Clear propositional statements attributed to God as authoritative teacher."
>
> HISTORICAL: "God reveals himself primarily in great deeds" as evidenced by the Bible.
>
> INNER EXPERIENCE: "Privileged inner experience of grace or communion with God."
>
> DIALECTICAL: A focus on the absolute transcendence of God. God "encounters human subjects" as he wills, concealing as often as revealing.
>
> NEW CONSCIOUSNESS: "An expansion of consciousness or shift of perspective."[12]

Dulles's argument was not received with wholehearted approval, as many critiqued his absolute rigidity and lack of flexibility. But his attempt offered a standard for Christian theology to argue against.

The first two categories have been most readily accepted as normative for many Christians, but as Terryl Givens points out, these categories do not include what most Latter-day Saints understand as revelation.[13] For example, Dulles disdains the category of inner experience because of its wide subjectivity, and he understands all biblical instances of conversation between God and humanity to be metaphorical. This is not how Joseph Smith (or the scripture he translated and produced) understood revelation. As Givens importantly argues, for Joseph Smith, revelation is "a personalized, dialogic exchange."[14] It is a conversation.

That is not to say that none in the Christian tradition understood revelation in a manner closer to Joseph Smith. We've already noted the radical Protestant Reformer Thomas Muntzer's insistence that if you were truly God's servant, you needed revelation. This impulse would continue as a persistent thread of Christian thought despite consistent efforts to limit or quash it. In the early Puritan Massachusetts Bay Colony, Ann Hutchinson wanted to read scripture in small groups in her home so the Spirit could speak directly to them, and they could learn together. She testified she was certain of her path because God had directly communicated with her through "immediate revelation"—she was exiled for it.[15] Quakers were consistently persecuted for their belief in ongoing revelation. These same questions about revelation continued to resurface, which, over time, would pave the way for Joseph Smith.

The role of a personal relationship with God was one of the issues at stake in the First Great Awakening—a label historians use to identify a period of great revival and reform in eighteenth-century Protestantism. Some Protestants, both in America and Europe, had begun to broaden their theology of revelation; a personal relationship with God was not only encouraged but could be considered essential. One of the famed fathers of the Great Awakening was Jonathan Edwards. Though he remains best known for his thoroughly Calvinist sermon "Sinners in the Hands of an Angry God," Edwards also taught that it was not an "unreasonable thing" to believe that if God cares for humanity, then God would speak to His people (though Edwards would limit that revelation—God would not reveal anything *new* in this way).[16] Edwards' contemporary and irritant, Bathesheba Kingsley, testified that the "immediate revelations from heaven" had encouraged her to steal her abusive husband's horse to "ride away on the Sabbath" to travel and preach the gospel.[17] Perhaps most comparable to Joseph Smith in terms of revelation, future Shaker leader Mother Ann Lee preached to her followers that they stood "on the threshold of a new age of revelation ... [and] their sacred knowledge could not be confined to the pages of a book."[18] Historian David Holland argues that many of Joseph's contemporaries similarly pined for a prophetic voice.[19] Though never generally accepted, this thread persisted.

Though few would acknowledge Joseph Smith as prophet, Joseph embodied this shared yearning for theology founded in direct communication and experience with God.

Historian Richard Bushman maintained, "At a time when the origins of Christianity were under assault by the forces of Enlightenment rationality, Joseph Smith returned modern Christianity to its origins in revelation."[20] As then-Elder Jeffrey Holland quoted Bushman, he added his witness, "Joseph Smith left us above all else the resolute legacy of divine revelation—not a single, isolated revelation without evidence or consequence, and not 'a mild sort of inspiration seeping into the minds of all good people' everywhere, but specific, documented, ongoing directions from God."[21]

A conversation.

The Revelations

Joseph Smith's first revelatory task was to be a translator of scripture. After he had "received the record of the Nephites," God gave him "power to translate through the mercy of God, by the power of God, the Book of Mormon" (1:29). More than a linguistic translator, Joseph relied on divine revelatory means to receive the translation. He never claimed a working knowledge of Reformed Egyptian. (See Mormon 9:32.) Joseph first expanded the known words of God in the Book of Mormon, revealed more missing scriptures, revised the Bible, and brought even more of Christ's words in his own revelations in the Doctrine and Covenants—enabling us to abound in scripture. With the Restoration, scripture was no longer a scarce commodity.

Let's examine the revelations to Joseph and others that were published—those that became official scripture—to see what they reveal about different modes and the medium through which those revelations come, and what they tell us about the potential for abundance.[22] As *The Joseph Smith Papers* suggests, Joseph developed a deep relationship with the revelations. "He marveled at them, defended them, and ensured that they were recorded, copied, edited, and published."[23] If we start with the mode of revelation, the different categories illuminate how the Lord worked with Joseph Smith and others as prophets and servants of God, and likewise, he models for us some of the many ways in which God speaks. He helps us to begin to recognize the possible scope of abundance. Though there is much more that we might discern from a quantitative look at the revelations, let's begin with some initial observations.

In chapter 2, we will explore the central role of asking questions, but here let me point out that by far the most frequent category of revelation is the word of the Lord that comes in response to a specific question. In fact, 65 percent of the revelations come in this manner. The second-largest

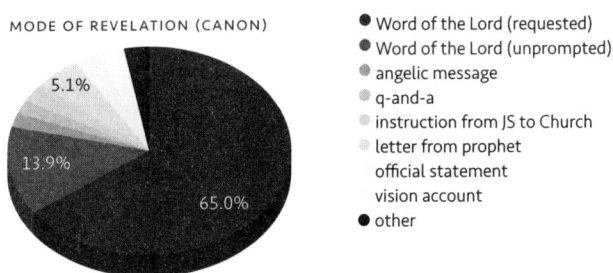

FIGURE 1.1. Modes of Revelation in the Doctrine and Covenants.

THE VOICE OF THE LORD AND JOSEPH SMITH 23

segment of revelations is the unprompted word of the Lord (nearly 14 percent), something that comes without a specific question—perhaps suggesting that truly hearing Him requires consistent vigilance so that we don't miss anything. If we're only listening when we've made a request, we will miss out on some of the revelations intended for us. Heavenly interventions into the prophet's life are another medium for divine learning and direction: visits of angelic messengers, visions where the veil is drawn back and he can see into eternity, and a translation coming from "parchment" detailing whether John the Beloved lived or died.[24] Joseph's own words mixed with those of the Lord in some of the revelations—the Lord's words as mediated by the prophet and the prophet's inspired direction—offered more guidance for the early Saints as well as for us today.

Let's likewise consider the audience of the revelations. Most of the revelations coming through the prophet are intended for a broad audience. Next, we have revelations to individuals and then revelations to a small group. God's

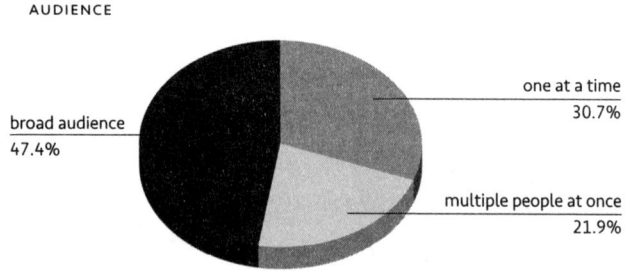

FIGURE 1.2. The Intended Audiences for Revelation in the Doctrine and Covenants.

TEXTUAL STYLES

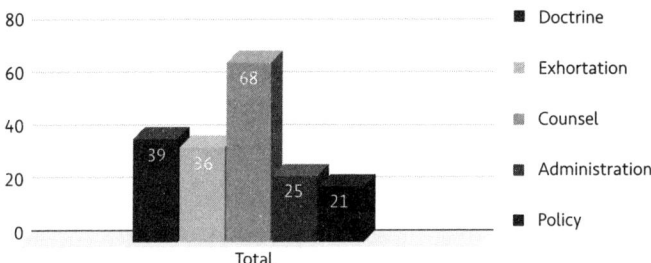

FIGURE 1.3. The Varying Textual Styles in the Doctrine and Covenants.

voice needs to reach a wide audience—"from afar" (1:1), and pragmatically, the easiest way to do this is with a megaphone speaking to a large group. Yet God still wants to speak to individuals as we reach out and petition. Other times it is a smaller group with a particular concern or question whom the Lord directs. We can receive individual revelation as well as revelation in community.

Moreover, just as the Lord doesn't always speak via the same medium, it isn't always the same kind of message. Some revelations fall into more than one category, which is why Figure 1.3 adds up to 189 when there are only 138 sections in the Doctrine and Covenants. There isn't a limit on the kinds of speaking the Lord does either.

The revealed word of the Lord can offer doctrinal propositions that help us collectively better understand the principles of the gospel and the foundations of the Church of Jesus Christ. The Lord can exhort and plead with us to change our ways—to do something or to stop doing something—either individually or as the body of the Church. The

Lord can counsel us and comfort us in times of worry, help us make decisions, or tell us we just need to choose. Matters of Church administrative structure as well as policies can be guided by the Lord. Most often, it seems, we just need a little guidance. The quantification of the revelations doesn't show the times responses aren't forthcoming and we are "waiting patiently on the Lord" (98:2).

The Lord's preface to the Doctrine and Covenants prioritizes Joseph Smith as a conduit for the Lord's commandments and provides a prophetic antidote to the calamity of the last days. While a better understanding of prophetic stewardship was clarified over time, hearing the voice of the Lord is never just the province of prophets (1:20). *All* have the possibility of hearing "specific, documented, ongoing directions from God"[25] individually "after the manner of their language" (1:17). Joseph's restoration of all things renewed an understanding that the voice of the Lord can speak to all. Will we do the work to hear?

2

Hearkening and Asking

Section 46

The Restoration began with a teenage boy with so many questions. Joseph Smith later described that as he grew, he "wanted to get Religion ... [he] wanted to feel and shout like the Rest but could feel nothing."[1] His religious experience didn't match that of others he knew, and he had concerns. According to Oliver Cowdery, local religious revivals encouraged Joseph that "*if* a Supreme being did exist," then he needed to know "that he was accepted of him."[2] In his earliest written account of his First Vision, he detailed how as he considered the overwhelming beauty of the earth and the universe, he realized that he believed that there was a God.[3] That realization brought more questions. He built on that belief and sought to develop his own faith—to understand where he stood before God and to seek forgiveness for his sins. Though we often focus on this vision as the beginning of his prophetic call, initially, this was Joseph asking God for forgiveness. He sought to know "that he had received a remission of his sins" (20:5). And over time he developed a relationship with God through an ongoing conversation with Him. We've considered what Joseph's seeking teaches us about the character of God.

Might Joseph's seeking also offer a revelatory pattern for us?

As was noted in the last chapter, a majority, 65 percent, of the revelations in the Doctrine and Covenants came in response to a question. By examining the frequency of the Lord's pleas in the revelations and giving more particular consideration to the initial and ending verses of section 46, this chapter explores the consummate importance of asking God. Joseph and other early Saints remarkably modeled this practice to ask God "in all things" (46:7). Joseph read scripture and took its promises seriously. He "lacked wisdom" and faithfully believed that God would "liberally" respond if he asked (James 1:5). This glorious answer provided a footing for the beginning of a life-long revelatory conversation with God and the founding of a community of like-minded seekers of God's will. As we'll see, Joseph sought God with what Moroni might label "real intent" or desire (Moroni 10:4).

A Desire to Hear

If revelation is available to all, then why is there a distinction between those who "will hear" and those who "may hear" (1:11)? Do we know what that means, or do we just assume we know what it means? In Joseph Smith's lifetime, "will" was defined as "to determine; to decide in the mind that something shall be done."[4] In this definition, will reflects agency—those who choose to hear the voice of the Lord, as we discussed in chapter 1. Another definition of will is "expressing desire"—they want to hear.[5] Moreover, President Russell M. Nelson pointed out that the Hebrew *shama,* which is translated as "hearken" in English, is "a strong verb that means to listen with the intent to obey."[6] "May hear" reminds us that all those who would use their agency to hear need the opportunity to choose to hearken (1:11). Part of God's revelatory project, made clear in the Restoration, is that everyone needs the possibility to choose.

Desire comes first. Elder Neal A. Maxwell explained, "desire denotes a real longing or craving. Hence righteous desires are much more than passive preferences or fleeting feelings."[7] So let's ask ourselves in all honesty: in our hearts do we want to know God's will concerning us? God blesses us according to our desires—even if it is just the desire to have a desire. The Lord will work with that. He will "let this desire work in [us]" (Alma 32:27). Nearly all of the revelations directed to individuals in the Doctrine and Covenants begin with a plea to hearken. If Joseph petitioned the Lord on those people's behalf, chances are that they already had some desire to know the will of God concerning them. Yet, if, like section 25 to Emma and sections 15 and 16 to two of the Whitmer brothers, their revelations from the Lord begin with "hearken," have they already accomplished it?

Perhaps in part. However, hearkening appears to be a constant process. To the Whitmer brothers, the Lord acknowledged that He knew the place of their hearts, looking back on the "many times you have desired of me to know that which would be of the most worth to you" (15:4, 16:4). And once again they asked for revelatory guidance, demonstrating their commitment over time. They truly wanted to know God's will, and the Lord wanted them to continue in that desire. Moreover, praying and desire are often aligned in scripture. Praying might be how we "offer up [our] most holy desires unto the Lord" (95:16; see also 58:44). Over and over again in scripture, God commands us to seek truth, wisdom, and divine guidance—the verb most frequently invoked is to ask.[8] Initiating that divine connection most frequently requires asking. We manifest our desire as we ask God.

A Question-Asking People

Elinor G. Jones was born into a multiracial family in Nashville in 1832, and she learned of the Church in Tennessee as a girl. Though we know little of her childhood, from her own words, we can see that asking questions helped her develop a deep relationship with God. Despite growing up with a mixed-race heritage in the South at the height of the oppressive violence of slavery, Elinor escaped the South, moving first to Ohio and then westward to Utah and California, where she passed as white and likely avoided the prejudice and limitations to which her sisters and brothers of African descent were subjected. In Utah, she was endowed and actively participated in her ward. In 1882, she taught the Young Women of her ward about prayer—a witness clearly cultivated through her own experience, pleading that they, too, seek through asking:

> If you will read the Bible, the Book of Mormon, and other good books, you will learn that all good and great people were those who prayed to God, for it is the only way to become good and great. And, my young friends, it is well for you to remember, while traveling on this journey of life, that there is no prison so dark, no pit so deep, no expanse so broad, that the Spirit of God cannot enter; and when all other privileges are denied us, we can pray, and God will hear us. No one can take this from us. But remember it is a most precious gift, it is something that must be cultivated; and when the still, small voice whispers, "Go and pray," you must obey; for if you do not, the Spirit will be grieved, and the voice in time becomes silent.

Her emphasis on prayer as a skill that must be cultivated is essential here. So, too, is what she said next, that God will receive even our clumsiest efforts at prayer with love and an answer, even if it's not the one we hoped for.

> Should you at any time find yourself overwhelmed with disappointment and sorrow, remember that although your prayers may be like the wailings of the most feeble infant, God, being more loving than the most tender mother, will hear and answer you. But we cannot say that he will always

answer according to the desires of your mind; but in his great wisdom he sees and knows what is for your best good and will answer according to his wisdom.[9]

Her own experience taught Elinor the necessity of asking questions to develop our relationship with God.

As Elder Uchtdorf reminds us, "We are a question-asking people. We have always been because we know that inquiry leads to truth. That is how the Church got its start, from a young man who had questions. In fact," he continued, "I'm not sure how one can discover truth without asking questions. In the scriptures, you will rarely discover a revelation that didn't come in response to a question.... Searching for answers to your questions can bring you closer to God, strengthening your testimony instead of shaking it."[10] Honest questions do not signal a lack of faith. Joseph Smith's theology of revelatory abundance suggests that questions are an important means to developing a relationship with God, building faith, and fulfilling our life mission. Just as a four-year-old with endless questions learns through the questions asked, questions also further develop the relationship between the asker and the asked. If I ignored all my niece's questions, it would be difficult for our relationship to grow and progress. Inquiry can lead to unfolding "mysteries which are great and marvelous" and help us better know how to help others and bring them to the truth (6:11).

Sometimes, revelations seem to answer a different question than the one originally asked, but the initiation of the conversation most often seems significant. In March of

1831, missionaries debated what to do with disruptive people attending their church meetings, and Joseph went to ask the Lord. Section 46, the revelation Joseph received in response, offers another model for divine learning and developing a relationship with God. The beginning of the revelation responded to Joseph's specific query while emphasizing a larger principle of revelatory abundance: a multitude of the ways that that abundance might be communicated to us, as well as what the Lord asks of us, and further emphasis on how we might guard against deception.

The first point demonstrated was their desire to understand. The elders didn't just move forward without trying to seek the Lord's guidance first; they didn't assure themselves they already knew the answer. They desired to know how God wanted them to deal with the situation and they asked the Prophet to ask the Lord on their behalf. The Lord responded with another reminder to "hearken" and then expanded the conversation to become a teaching opportunity. In the process, the Lord revealed far more for their "profit and learning" than their initial ask (46:1). The Lord established the larger principle first: the Spirit is always most important and "has always been." Only then did the Lord answer their specific query: "never cast anyone out" (46:3). Then He repeated that counsel two more times to be sure it sank in. The only caveat offered is that people be "earnestly seeking the kingdom" (46:5–6), opening the possibility to remove someone if there is true disruption.

Let's think about how to apply this scripture. The Lord taught the Saints in Kirtland a larger principle that the Spirit must always prevail in meetings and in our lives. Though we may be attached to "those things that are written" (46:2), whether that be a program for a meeting, or a talk, or a plan for our lives, the most important guide is the Spirit and, on our part, openness to revelatory abundance. If the communication that comes is not what you expect, are you ready to throw out the talk or lesson you've spent a week on if the Spirit directs? What if it means that your carefully orchestrated plan for your life looks more confusing and messier than you're comfortable with? What if the communication comes through someone or something you did not consider a medium for revelation? Part of asking and expecting that God wants to communicate with us is that all bets are off. Plans might be amended, transformed, or thrown out.

The Lord then reiterates the absolute necessity of asking. "Ye are commanded in all things to ask of God, who giveth liberally" (46:7). A commandment? We would not be surprised with an invitation from the Lord to ask him for direction but classifying asking, instead, as a commandment changes things. As Professors Stephen Robinson and Dean Garrett considered, "It is common for members to ask of God when they lack blessings or knowledge, but verse 7 makes it clear we are to pray and to ask for God's involvement in our affairs. To view ourselves as spiritually self-sufficient or as in some degree independent of God is not a virtue, nor is it a feeling that we are doing just fine by merely touching base with him occasionally. To communicate with God regularly in all aspects of our lives is not just good advice or a sweet invitation; it is a *commandment*."[11] That should help us consider just how the Lord categorizes the importance of asking questions: He commands us to do it.

Most often, revelation comes when we initiate the process and trust in God and God's character to communicate "liberally" to those who seek, and then recognize the response, "that which the Spirit testifies unto you" (46:7). If the heavens are opened, we need to keep asking questions, and we just might need to brace ourselves for change. Heeding the Spirit has the potential to change our whole selves as the Spirit writes in the "fleshy tables of our hearts" (2 Corinthians 3:3). Motivation for the revelation matters—the desire matters. We choose who writes on our hearts and how we find our center. The Lord continued, "even so I would that ye should do in all holiness of heart, walking uprightly before me, considering the end of your salvation, doing all things with prayer and thanksgiving" (46:7). Sometimes we get in our own way when our motives are not centered on knowing God's will concerning us; sometimes others get in our way. Now, it could be "evil spirits, or doctrines of devils" intentionally blocking our way, or it could be merely the "commandments of men" that obstruct us. There are many potential hazards in our way to living in revelatory abundance that we will further consider in chapter 7.

Help from the Holy Spirit

Now, lest we feel intimidated and concerned that we're never wholly holy as we struggle through mortal mud, in almost the same breath, section 46 sets up gifts of the Spirit as a means to help us, "lest [we] are deceived" (46:8). The revelation acknowledges that it is not perfect application but having the desire that is most important for us to access that help. The aid of the Spirit is given "for the benefit of those who love me and keep all my commandments." Before we panic, thinking we will never perfectly love God nor perfectly keep *all* the commandments, the all-important caveat comes: the promise is liberally applied to all those who successfully love and keep all the commandments (if such mortals existed) *and* to those of us "who seeketh to do so" (46:9). Our attempt, no matter how human and limited, is important. The Lord wants us to ask and wants us to try. After a suggestive list of potential gifts of the Spirit in section 46, the end of the revelation returns to the commandment to ask God. All are promised at least one gift of the Spirit—a gift or gifts we can expand by developing our relationship with God through asking questions.

In the late nineteenth century, Emma Anderson Lilijenquist received a calling to attend a class in obstetrics and nursing in Salt Lake City. She lived a considerable distance to the north in Cache Valley, and the classes required her to be away from her family for six months. She was pregnant with her fourth child at her graduation. None of this felt expected or easy for her, but as she was set apart, Apostle John Henry Smith promised that if she "lived right [she] should always know what to do in the case of any difficulties." As she wrote her reminiscences, she considered how she had been led by the Lord:

> That promise has been fulfilled to the very letter. Many times when one of my patients were seriously ill I have asked my Heavenly Father for assistance and in every case it was given to me. One in particular was a lady who had just given birth to a baby and hemorrhage set in. The husband called the doctor but he did not realize that it was so serious. I placed my hands upon her head and asked the Lord to help us. The hemorrhage ceased and I did the necessary things for her. When the doctor arrived he said he could hardly believe what had happened but said I had done exactly what he would have done.[12]

The Spirit offered Emma help beyond her previous knowledge to bless and save the life of another, not unlike President Russell M. Nelson's feeling the Spirit guide him to know how to fix a patient's faulty heart valve.[13] Though it wasn't something she expected or planned, Emma asked for God's help, followed the Spirit to bless and serve others, and fulfilled her mission.

We need to be open to God's voice to us and then trust in His direction. This is not always easy, even for people we regard as stalwarts in the faith. In the early days of the Church, the Prophet surprised new member Newel K. Whitney with a calling to be a bishop in Kirtland (72:8). Newel told Joseph, "I cannot see a bishop in myself." Joseph told him to not just trust in his word alone, but to go to God. Newel prayed and heard "a voice from heaven," which told him, "Thy strength is in me."[14] He knew that it was God's will and that he would have God's help. It didn't matter that he couldn't imagine it; God saw a bishop in him despite his inexperience. God knows our capacity and our potential better than our friends, spouses, siblings, or parents and better than we know ourselves. God doesn't leave us alone in this, as Spencer Fluhman reminded us, "You might think of yourself as seeking God ... but, in truth, He has been seeking you."[15] Or, as Elder Patrick Kearon pointedly expressed, "God is in relentless pursuit of you."[16]

3

Scripture Abounds

Sections 20, 76, and 138

While most other nineteenth-century religious leaders published commentaries on scripture, Joseph Smith's first material product of revelation brought to light more scripture: stories of ancient people in the New World as they interacted with God and a post-mortal Christ. Most people's first interaction with the restored gospel came through the Book of Mormon.[1] As they encountered the Book of Mormon they had to decide—was the biblical text sufficient and final, as some of their Protestant traditions had taught them? Or was there more? Could scripture be abundant?

Many were converted to the idea of more scripture before they ever knew the man who produced that book by "the gift and power of God."[2] William W. Phelps dated his conversion from the day he received a Book of Mormon. Though it was some time before he met Joseph and was baptized, for him and many others, the first stage of his conversion to the Restoration was based on this new book of scripture.[3] Though conversion came differently for each of the early Saints, for many, the divine inspiration of the Book of Mormon was confirmed for them experientially through the Spirit as they read. They heard God's voice through new scripture.

The idea of more scripture was a punchline for outsiders, and the source of the initially pejorative nickname "Mormon," yet believers grasped the nickname because it testified of the possibility of adding even more scripture to their Bible-drenched world. Then God spoke again, and Joseph provocatively dictated even more of God's words. This act further shattered allegiance to *sola scriptura,* the foundational Protestant belief in the Bible as the infallible and singular truth. God still wanted to communicate with His children. This chapter considers the role of scripture as God's word—a testament that God has always spoken. We will consider scripture as a subset of the larger principle of revelation at the Church's founding through section 20 and then explore how it serves as fuel to ignite divine learning and as a medium through which we might more readily hear God's voice to us as we consider what practices led to the visions recorded in sections 76 and 138.

New Scripture

In founding documents known as the Articles and Covenants, the new Church of Christ assumed the Bible and the Book of Mormon as canon, official scripture considered "genuine and inspired"[4] (20:9–11). By the nineteenth century, some European scholars of biblical criticism had begun to question the divinity of the Bible, stacking up problems with the text. For some, this led to a dismissal of the divine in the text. In the opposite direction, the Book of Mormon reinforced the divine voice of the Bible, even if Joseph Smith would later acknowledge its limitations. A part of these founding documents, section 20 makes a theological argument about the power and enduring importance of the Bible. According to this section, the Book of Mormon testifies that "the holy scriptures are true" (20:11). As modern Latter-day Saints, we might read "the holy scriptures" as what we call the standard works today, our canon. Yet in the nineteenth century in America, the idea of having many different scriptures was an aberration. (This is a radical conceit of Joseph Smith's claim to new scripture and open heavens.) In that era and in the centuries prior to it, "the scriptures" were the Bible.

If we read "the scriptures" in 20:11 as the Bible, this means the Doctrine and Covenants argues that rather than competing with the Bible, the Book of Mormon supports it. Despite mounting difficulties apparent in the human construction of the biblical text, it remains "true." We could write another book on what we mean when we say something is true, but here it seems the Book of Mormon substantiates the divine value of the Bible. The Book of Mormon confirms that it was part of God's character to speak and communicate with His children in the New World as in the Old, in the present as in the past, near and far.

The task was to communicate with those children. Yet, at the same time as the voice of the Lord reaches out to all, the text acknowledges the intermediate steps necessary to hear the voice of the Lord through scripture. A process and method are necessary to receive the word of God in scripture. Jesus doesn't snap His fingers, and scripture appears ex nihilo. The voice of the Lord's revelatory project rarely came directly from the Lord's mouth; it was always mediated by the Spirit and "by the mouths of my disciples" (1:4). Revelations came through Joseph in language familiar to Joseph. And though Joseph is still the means through which these new scriptures came, and there are similarities in the echoes, allusions, and quotations of the King James Version (it is clearly the Smith family's mother tongue)—the Book of Mormon and the new revelations arrive in different voices. Then, additional "servants of the Lord" acted as scribes to write down the words Joseph spoke to practically enable the dissemination of God's word.

As an "active participant," scribe Emma Smith described the process as a "marvel and a wonder."[5] Oliver Cowdery deemed his time as Joseph's scribe "as days never to be forgotten."[6] There is something holy and valuable in both the mouthpiece mediating the word and the ones providing the conduit for circulation enabling further reception of more of God's words. As John Whitmer acted as a scribe, the Lord reminded him that he was reliant on the Spirit to write (47:4). Others were given the task to "preserve [scripture] in safety" and to be "stewards over scripture" (42:56 and 70:3). These stewards likewise over time edited the revelations and prepared them for publication.

To disseminate more of the word to more of God's people, the Saints needed their own press. The first effort to systematically publish Joseph's revelations came in 1832 with the creation of the *Evening and Morning Star*. Its prospectus described it to "be devoted to the revelations of God as made known to his servants by the Holy Ghost, at sundry times since the creation of man, but more especially in these last days."[7] As W. W. Phelps published the newspaper, he likewise worked on the first full collection of Joseph's revelations to be published, initially titled *The Book of Commandments*. This would later become *The Doctrine and Covenants*.

A Great and Marvelous Word

As we begin to read the published revelations, we soon encounter some repetition. Many of these sections are given to individuals who desired Joseph to inquire "of the Lord concerning" them.[8] Five of these revelations begin with biblical language from the Book of Revelation, looking forward to "a great and marvelous work about to come forth" (4:1, 6:1, 11:1, 12:1, 14:1). Over time, this language has been interpreted in various ways, often as referring to the Restoration in general with a particular connection to the call to missionary work that comes in section 4—the archetypal call to missionary work. However, the other four instances of the "great and marvelous work about to come forth" in the Doctrine and Covenants are followed with language from Hebrews that "the word of God is quick and powerful" (Heb. 4:12). These instances connect the great and marvelous work to the word of God. In this way, the new scripture is an essential facet of the work of the Restoration.

Then the text lays out characteristics of God's word— it is "quick and powerful and sharper than a two-edged sword" (6:2, 11:2, 12:2, 14:2). We might interpret "quick" as fast, leaning toward a battle-ready interpretation, but the old English defines quick as "living, endowed with life, animate."[9] "Sharp" can describe something destructive, but it can likewise point to something that does its job effectively. The *Oxford English Dictionary* describes sharpness as something "well adapted" or "punctual," "arriving at the right time."[10] God's word can be all these things. God's word might be fast, it might be slow, but it will be what we need. It will arrive on time, and its power is in its living connection with the divine.

Elizabeth Haven was one of those for whom the word arrived right on time. She joined a church when she was twenty, and she read the Bible consistently but felt something missing. Not long after, her cousins, Brigham Young and Willard Richards, visited and preached the restored gospel and gave her a Book of Mormon. "She read attentively," and "the Spirit of God rested upon [her]." She described feeling "convinced to say in [her] heart, 'This is the way I long sought and mourned because I found it not.'"[11] I love the imagery of mourning something you didn't know you were missing. After two years of immersing herself in new scripture, Elizabeth Haven described how it offered her a new lens through which she now saw her life more clearly. She testified to a friend who would soon join her in Nauvoo, "The understanding and knowledge we have of the scriptures makes friends and everything appear in a very different light to me."[12] Think of how much an effect light can have. I love the golden hour of the day as the sun is setting when everything the light touches seemingly glows. Scripture changed how she saw and understood her world—it can do the same for us.

In the Restoration, there was simply more scripture to take in. Don't underestimate the work required to begin to know a 598-page Book of Mormon and then an ever-growing collection of new revelations. In the early revelations, the Lord repeatedly instructs individuals that they "seek to obtain my word before [they] declare my word." Their "time [should] be devoted to studying the scriptures," which are "given of me for your instruction" and for "the salvation of mine own elect" (11:21 26:1, 33:16, 35:20). Though the definition of the elect has been much debated in the history of Christianity, in the fall of 1830 the Lord defined the elect for the Restoration as those who hear the voice of God and "harden not their hearts" (29:7). If we claim a relationship with God and we want to hear God's voice to us, we can encounter that voice through scripture. Like Elizabeth, we can experience scripture as a lens that makes "everything appear in a different light" to us.

The word of God takes on salvific properties if we take it

in and write it on our hearts. If we have made Melchizedek priesthood covenants in the House of the Lord, a significant element of the oath and covenant of the priesthood is that we center ourselves on revelation. We're taught to "give diligent heed to the words of eternal life" and "live by every word that proceedeth forth from the mouth of God" (84:43–44). A few verses later in that same section, we are reminded how "lightly" we often treat scripture, and the Lord admonishes us to immerse ourselves in scripture and let it change us, "not only to say, but to do" (84:57).

Scripture and Visions

In several instances in the revelations in the Doctrine and Covenants, visions become a significant source of salvific revealed knowledge, yet none of these visions just popped out of nowhere. Remember that a majority of revelations (65%) came in response to a question. In the case of "The Vision" laid out by Joseph and Sidney Rigdon in 1832, their own studying of scriptures and a dialogic conversation with God led to the vision (76). As they worked on Joseph's translation of the Bible, they came upon John 5:29, which spoke of "the resurrection of life" and "the resurrection of damnation." They didn't understand. And when they asked, the Spirit enabled them to understand. They wrote, "this caused us to marvel, for it was given to us of the Spirit." While they were yet basking in the experience of receiving a divine response to their question and meditating on it, "the Lord touched the eyes of our understandings and they were opened, and the glory of the Lord shone round about" (76:15–20). Taking the time to meditate on the revelation that they had received through the Spirit enabled them to see. And they saw far more than they could have anticipated—a panoptic vision of the three degrees of glory and the whole plan of salvation.

The contents of the vision were so significant that twice during the vision, the Lord commanded them to "write the vision" (76:28, 49). After the vision concluded, they followed those commands, as well as the command not to write those things which were "not lawful for man to utter; neither is man capable to make them known." Joseph described those things that could "only be seen and understood by the power of the Holy Spirit" by those who love God and purify themselves, and then He individually "grants the privilege of seeing and knowing for themselves" (76:115–117). If we return to the Greek word translated as revelation, *apokalypsis* describes those mysteries hidden from our sight; they can be uncovered or continue to be hidden according to the divine will—therefore, revelation can reveal as much as it conceals. Not all are prepared for all revelations. Joseph and Sidney were prepared to receive even more, and only individually does the Lord determine who "may be able to bear his presence in the world of glory" (76:118). As we will discuss in the next chapter, we need prophets who are ready to receive more than we are ready to receive. We need those who can see farther than we can currently see.

Similarly, Joseph F. Smith's 1918 vision of the spirit world was initiated by the studying of scripture and asking questions. Being surrounded by death was not new for

Joseph F., whose father Hyrum and uncle Joseph were killed when he was five. His mother, Mary, died when he was thirteen. This trend would continue and was particularly oppressive in 1918. Frail himself, he mourned the recent death of a son, Hyrum, and then Hyrum's wife, Ida. Meanwhile, World War I raged, and a worldwide flu pandemic proliferated. He "sat in [his] room pondering over the scriptures" as the pandemic hit Utah. He began to reflect on "the great atoning sacrifice" of the Savior and remembered the writings of Peter to the early Christian saints. He turned to 1 Peter 3–4. This was not his first time reading it; as he put it, his "mind reverted to the writings of the apostle Peter." This meant he was already familiar with these verses. But something was different this time when he was "greatly impressed, more than [he] had ever been before," as the verses detailed how, after His death, Christ "went and preached unto the spirits in prison" (138:1–6; 1 Peter 3:18–20). Not unlike the earlier experience of Joseph and Sidney, as Joseph F. pondered these verses, "the eyes of [his] understanding were opened, and the Spirit of the Lord rested upon [him], and [he] saw the hosts of the dead, both small and great" (138:11).

In both instances, scripture initiated a glorious view. These men were given answers to their questions through the Spirit. As they meditated and marveled at the responses, God pulled back the veil and allowed them not only to understand the answers to their specific questions but much more. They were given a glimpse into eternity. This "more" is possible for us as well. Studying scripture, pondering, meditating, and immersing ourselves in scripture can lead to much more. How often do we stop with an answer to our initial question when the Lord is ready to give us more?

Studying Scripture

If we want to receive the word of God, we might consider the difference between *reading* scripture and *studying* scripture. Both models we just reviewed included pondering and meditating as a significant part of the revelatory process. Consider Elder Todd Christofferson's counsel,

> When I say 'study,' I mean something more than reading.... I see you sometimes reading a few verses, stopping to ponder them, carefully reading the verses again, and as you think about what they mean, praying for understanding, asking questions in your mind, waiting for spiritual impressions, and writing down the impressions and insights that come so you can remember and learn more. Studying in this way, you may not read a lot of chapters or verses in a half hour, but you will be giving place in your heart for the word of God, and He will be speaking to you.[13]

Just as it takes time to learn how God speaks to us, learning the language of scripture is a part of this process that comes through study—through immersing ourselves in scripture. It's more than just ticking off a box and reading some assigned verses. For conversion, we need more.

The language of scripture can sometimes seem foreign to us, but just like any new language, immersing ourselves makes a difference. When I was in the Missionary Training

Center, our teachers pled with us to only speak Spanish. It was difficult, but the more we submerged ourselves in the new language, the sooner it became familiar. Complete immersion once I arrived in Argentina did not feel so uncomfortable for long. As we slow down to try and understand individual words and phrases in scripture and not just assume we know what it says, the language of scripture becomes a part of us. Moreover, the language of scripture builds upon itself. Paraphrases, echoes, and allusions to other scripture are essential to the fabric of scripture—these connections are essential to its character and how it operates in the world.

Early Black Latter-day Saints Jane Manning James and Samuel Chambers understood this well. Both developed a remarkable relationship with scripture that welded them to the Restoration despite trying circumstances. For them, Restoration scripture highlighted the full emancipatory promises of the gospel that they did not yet experience within their Latter-day Saint community. Jane described her scripture practice, "I used to read in the Bible so much and in the Book of Mormon and Revelations." As her eyesight dimmed, she lamented the loss of reading scripture herself, yet she had already developed a relationship with scripture. Echoes of and allusions to Restoration scripture pepper her autobiography. In 1884, she wrote to Church President John Taylor "concerning her future salvation." The letter was short and yet included multiple allusions to each book of the standard works. She used scripture to argue for the extension of priesthood and temple blessings to her and her Black

IMAGE 2. Jane Mannings James (ca. 1862–1895), by James Martin. Image courtesy of the Church History Library.

sisters and brothers that they were as yet denied.[14] When Jane sat for a photographic portrait in the 1870s, she chose how she wanted to be remembered, and Jane chose a book to include in her portrait under her left arm, one that looks remarkably like an 1870s Book of Mormon. Perhaps Jane wanted to highlight her literacy, perhaps Jane wanted to illustrate her own relationship with scripture to the world.[15]

Samuel Chambers was born "in a condition of slavery" in Mississippi. He met missionaries and was baptized as an enslaved thirteen-year-old in 1844. Not taught to read, Samuel learned to memorize scripture as he attended Baptist church services with other enslaved people nearby. The process of memorization seemed to mark scripture upon his soul. After emancipation, he gathered with the Saints in Utah in 1870. Samuel had shared the gospel with his wife Amanda and her extended family, and all of them joined him in Utah. He taught himself to read, while Amanda used McGuffey Readers to teach herself, and they continued to immerse themselves in scripture. The Chamberses had "mormon books, nothing but mormon books" in their home and shared those books with others.[16]

Samuel was not ordained to a priesthood office as was Elijah Able and a handful of other Black Saints. He was called as an assistant to the deacons' quorum—at this point still generally an adult priesthood quorum. In weekly quorum meetings, Chambers testified twenty-nine times over a three-year period.[17] We see him likening scripture unto himself and focusing on the emancipatory promise of Restoration scripture as he testified. Samuel frequently and specifically quoted, paraphrased, alluded to, and echoed scripture—the Book of Mormon more than anything else. Though he never explicitly petitioned for priesthood ordination, he implicitly demonstrated his worthiness to receive more blessings and responsibilities as a lively member of Christ's church.[18]

On a December night in 1874, Samuel shared his testimony with the quorum, paraphrasing a scriptural promise. "I was born in a condition of slavery, and received the gospel in that condition," he said. "I realized I had done right. I received the spirit of God.... It is not only to the Gentiles but also to the African, for I am of that race."[19] As Chambers testified of his experience with God, the witness he had personally received, he "likened" scripture unto himself and expanded the scriptural promise that the gospel would be taken to the Gentiles, and also to his own people (1 Nephi 22:9; Doctrine and Covenants 112:4). As Samuel likened scripture unto himself, he, like Jane, found a place for himself in the Restoration and demonstrated his fitness to receive more truth and more responsibility among the people of God. Reading and studying the word of God prepares us for exhorting and expounding scripture, teaching each other in community, and for better understanding who we are to God no matter our immediate context.

In the revelations, the Lord defines the act of presenting, detailing, and interpreting scripture as simply something that saintly people do. Expounding and exhorting scripture is specific to the duties of elders, priests, and deacons (20:42, 46, 59, 59) as well as the Lord's specific counsel to Emma Smith—she is to "expound scripture and exhort the church" (25:7). While there were female exhorters in Emma's former reformed Methodist tradition, called to testify of Christ and inspire others to improve their lives, expounding was something reserved for male ministers.[20] Despite any discomfort she might have felt, expounding (explaining and interpreting) scripture for the Church was one of the tasks the Lord gave her. The Lord's words to Emma were also "unto all" (25:16). As Elder Neal A. Maxwell was fond of saying, "For too long in the Church, the men have been the theologians while the women have been the Christians."[21] While this is an additional reminder of the central importance of charity for all of us who call ourselves disciples, it reminds us that the Lord desires all of us to be scriptorians and theologians. This is not just the province of the ivory tower, or Church leaders, or "the men"; it is the responsibility of us all. We all need more of God's voice. Will we hearken to God's voice in the abundance of ways that He continues to show us that He is still speaking? And then, will we help others likewise hear His voice?

While Joseph confidently moved away from a Protestant conception of *sola scriptura,* he continued to expand the saints' sense of scripture itself in the fall of 1831. Speaking to missionaries, the Lord exhorted them to "speak as they are moved upon by the Holy Ghost." He then shattered any sense of scripture as finite: "whatsoever they shall speak when moved upon by the Holy Ghost shall be scripture" (68:3–4). This did not abolish the idea of canon: official scripture would still be presented before the body of the

Church and voted on by the law of common consent (26:2, 28:13). However informal this category of scripture may be, this further negates any sense of scripture as a scarce commodity as it aligns with the promise of the Lord's preface given the same day, that all "might speak in the name of the Lord God" (1:20). Acting in concert with the inspiration of the Holy Ghost becomes a remarkable gift, one that requires learning and growing and practice. In the Restoration, the gifts of prophecy and scripture are the provenance of prophets—the prophet had a unique and special role in obtaining revelation for the Church as a whole. But they are likewise part of that growing revelatory abundance available to all.

4

My Servant, Joseph Smith, Jr.

Sections 28 and 43

We met Newel Whitney at the end of chapter 2 when he received his call to be the bishop in Kirtland. Although he had only known the Prophet Joseph for a few months, he trusted Joseph as a prophet. In a vision, Joseph had seen Newel and Elizabeth Whitney praying for a prophet before he ever came to Ohio, and "Joseph, the Prophet" knew Newel by name before he'd been introduced. Their relationship continued to develop from there. Yet, Joseph did not ask him to rely only on his prophetic position to know that the call was from God. He wanted Newel to verify that this was the Lord's will through Newel's own personal communication with God. God not only offered a second witness to Newel that he should be the bishop despite his inexperience in the

Church, but also revealed to Joseph the capacity that God could see in this recent convert.[1] Both channels of revelation were important, and they worked in tandem—the prophetic witness and the personal one.

In the preface to the Doctrine and Covenants, the Lord's voice speaks to Joseph Smith, introducing the collection of revelations to offer "a voice of warning," a counter to "calamity" (1:4, 17). The text points to a future apocalyptic day when "the arm of the Lord shall be revealed." It is a day void of prophets, full of apostasy, rebellion, and broken covenants. This calamity is defined by the community's gradual wandering from the covenant relationship with God and beginning to create and worship idols (1:9–16). As my divinity school Hebrew Bible professor argued, everyone has religion—where they choose to place their focus and time—it just isn't God for everyone. The children of Israel wanted a god that they could see and touch, which should sound familiar to us; we all, at times, make God in *our* own image. Yet it is within the power of God to foresee the calamity of apostasy and lost relationship and to provide a preemptive antidote. This chapter will consider the necessity of a prophet as we examine the tension between personal revelation and the prophetic mantle through two critical moments when the Lord established the order in revelation. Abundance does not equal chaos.

An Antidote to Chaos and Calamity

The Lord says, "Wherefore, I the Lord, knowing the calamity which should come upon the inhabitants of the earth, called upon my servant Joseph Smith, Jun., and spake unto him from heaven, and gave him commandments" (1:17). The antidote to chaos and calamity is a prophet to whom the Lord speaks. In calling His servant Joseph Smith, the Lord renewed certain lines of divine communication, such as the covenant, priesthood authority, and later prophetic succession. The Lord's disciples, in turn, continue to communicate these warnings and guidance to others. One of the tasks of discipleship is to warn—to receive God's words and pass them on to others. In that opening section of the Doctrine and Covenants, note that the "voice of warning" comes through "the mouths of my disciples, whom I have chosen in these last days" (1:4). Whether our chaos is collective or individual, present or future, the Lord offers to quell the calamity through communication with prophets, His servants, and His disciples.

Many scriptures attest that the Lord puts down chaos. Isaiah prophesied of Jehovah's ability to conquer Tiamat, the goddess of chaos, and her monstrous servants Rahab and Leviathan, who promulgated chaos across the seas (Isaiah 51:9; 2 Nephi 8:9–11). (Water often exemplifies chaos in scripture.) In the New Testament, while a tempest raged and the disciples feared, Jesus slept. When they awoke Him, He quelled the raging storm and the terror in their hearts with the words, "Peace, be still" (Mark 4:36–41). After a night of unsuccessful fishing on their own, the Lord told Peter and the others to fish in a different place, and their haul was so plentiful that "their net brake" (Luke 5:1–7). In our own time, whether the Lord eradicates the chaos or helps us steer through it, He knows how to direct us. Likewise, the Lord called upon Joseph Smith as the means to help us navigate the chaos (1:17).

As Joseph and five others organized the Church of Christ in 1830, he received revelations that established his prophetic role as key to the Church's foundation (sections 20–21). God gave him "power from on high," and he translated by the "gift and power of God," revealing ancient records to a modern audience (20:8). The first revelation to the newly organized church said that Joseph was to be known as "a seer, a translator, a prophet" (21:1). All of these roles rotated around revelation. While Joseph had many responsibilities and tasks, relaying the Lord's words to His people would be foundational. As a modern-day prophet, he began to lead the church and communicate more of God's words. Yet along with the prophet's revelatory roles, in that first revelation to the new Church, the Lord laid out our responsibilities as fellow saints, directing us to "give heed to all [Joseph's] words and commandments ... as if from my own mouth, in all patience and faith" (21:5).

Personal and Prophetic Lines of Communication

Over time, the Lord further established the role of Joseph Smith as the prophet of the Church. Like Moses, Joseph was the one "appointed to receive commandments and revelations" for the community as a whole (28:2). However, this led to some tension: one man was designated to be a prophet, yet all Saints had the possibility to receive revelation. Reflecting the new American republic's democratic emphasis, most American denominations at the time functioned democratically. Many of the early Saints assumed that the Restoration would likewise function that way. Jesus's words in the Sermon on the Mount wove through multiple revelations, reflecting the centrality of communication to the character of God: "Ask, and it shall be given you;... seek, and ye shall find; knock, and it shall be opened unto you: For every one that asketh receiveth; and he that seeketh findeth; and to him that knocketh it shall be opened. Or what man is there of you, whom if his son ask bread, will he give him a stone?" (Matthew 7:7–9). The Lord's preface opened the possibility for *all* "to speak in the name of God" (1:20).

Just months after the organization of the Church of Christ, this tension was manifest as Hiram Page, a Whitmer brother-in-law and one of the eight witnesses to the Book of Mormon, began to receive revelations through his seer stone that he believed were for the whole church, including the location of Zion. Newel Knight described "quite a roll of papers full of these revelations, and many in the church were led astray by them."[2] Joseph's first inclination was not to do anything until a planned church conference. However, the need soon became more critical. Many in his inner circle, the supportive Whitmer family and Oliver Cowdery, Joseph's right-hand man and future brother-in-law of Page, believed the revelations. Oliver urged Joseph to ask the Lord for a revelation, and Joseph resolved that yes, "it would be best to enquire of the Lord concerning such a matter."[3] With Joseph as the mediator of the Lord's word, the revelation was given to Oliver to resolve his questions about Page's revelatory role and to reaffirm Joseph's role as prophet and revelator. The Lord established that "no one shall be appointed to receive commandments and revelations in this church excepting my servant, Joseph Smith, Jun." Joseph was to the modern church as Moses was to the children of Israel (28:2). The Lord tasked Oliver to bring the true revelation to Hiram, "between he and thee alone." In this private setting, Oliver should "tell him that those things which he hath written from that stone are not of me and that Satan deceiveth him" (28:11). To Page's credit, we don't hear of this moment again; he must have heeded that chastisement. However, the theme of not being deceived winds throughout the first fifty sections of the Doctrine and Covenants.

Lest Oliver worry that this stamped out all possibilities for individual revelation, the Lord quickly reaffirmed Oliver's own ability to receive revelation to speak, teach, and write, but added that Joseph had "the keys of the mysteries and revelations which I sealed" (28:7). When Oliver spoke or wrote with inspiration it would *not* be "by way of commandment, but by wisdom" (28:5). This moment reveals more about the principle of revelation and the order inherent in the principle—we need a prophet, but we likewise need our own personal revelation. This introduces two essential channels of revelation: a "personal line" and a "priesthood line" of communication. Then-Elder Oaks called both "essential."[4] When the two lines are working in balance, it is a blessing, helping us "to achieve the growth that is the purpose of mortal life." Elder Oaks taught that if our religious practice relies too heavily on the personal line, "individualism erases the importance of divine authority." But if we depend too much on the priesthood line, we fail to grow as individuals. "The children of God need both lines to achieve their eternal destiny," he said. "The restored gospel teaches both, and the restored Church provides both."[5]

Individual revelation and a prophetic voice can work together rather than devolve into the chaos that Martin Luther feared. Joseph's prophetic mantle is the antidote to chaos, not a new way to introduce more calamity into the world. Sometimes, it is tricky to balance the prophet's word and our own revelation, but always worth it if we want to navigate chaos. As the revelation continues, the Lord clarifies the inherent order in divine communication, an order that is held up in turn by the community's "common consent" and the "prayer of faith" (28:13).

The next year, a similar, likely more public, challenge to Joseph's prophetic mantle came from a woman known as Mrs. Hubble. According to John Whitmer's history, she "professed to be a prophetess of the Lord. And professed to have many revelations, and knew that the Book of Mormon was true; and that she should become a teacher in the Church of Christ."[6] Though Whitmer's description leaves many questions, it suggests that, like Hiram Page, Mrs. Hubble, too, believed that she was receiving revelations for the Church as a whole. Mrs. Hubble seems to have departed the Saints quite quickly, but nine months later, detractor Ezra Booth wrote, "the barbed arrow which she left in the hearts of some, is not yet eradicated."[7] Ezra was trying to ridicule Joseph and his claim to prophetic privilege, but he also revealed the difficulty the Saints had in discerning which voices would be nourishing for their souls. A barbed arrow is effective because it damages on its way in and on its way out. Such damage can be healed, but it will require time and care.

The Lord's response in section 43 can help us avoid those destructive arrows. It emphasizes the essential elements of order in revelation and also highlights our agency to choose to listen; it's significant that the revelation once again begins with a call to "hearken." The Lord then asks the Saints to remember their recent past. Collectively, they had just received "the Law," the law of consecration, through Joseph, the one "appointed unto you to receive commandments and revelations from my hand," a few days earlier (43:2). One of the most consequential revelations of the Restoration, the law of consecration would shape their understanding of the gospel: both their temporal and spiritual lives were to be centered on the Lord. And now, so quickly, they were tempted to listen to another's claim to authority with Mrs. Hubble. "And this shall you know assuredly—that there is none other appointed unto you to receive commandments and revelations until he be taken, if he abide in me." Here, the Lord lays down a model. The prophet is the one to receive revelations for the Church for as long as the Saints have him. The caveat, "if he abide in me," acknowledges that Joseph can fall; the revelations consistently acknowledge Joseph's humanity and his human fallibility. However, the Lord continues asking them to remember how Joseph received that striking revelation, and then asks them to remember their own experiential witness. If they know he is a prophet, then they need to listen to him and not to contending voices. "There is none other appointed," the Lord makes clear (43:3).

A Personal Witness

Receiving our own witness of the prophet becomes a reciprocal requirement. The prophet needs our prayers and our patience. We need the Spirit to testify to us of the prophet's divine call and, most particularly, to the prophet's testimony of Christ. For Joseph, "the fundamental principle of our religion is the testimony of the apostles and prophets concerning Jesus Christ, 'that he died, was buried, and rose again the third day, and ascended up into heaven.'"[8] Every other part of our religion are "appendages" to that central premise. Joseph said he published this to "save myself the trouble of repeating the same a thousand times over and over again."[9] His repetition reinforces the critical necessity of receiving our own witness of the call of prophets and apostles, and their testimony of Christ becomes primary as we develop our own testimony of the Savior.

It was for Mary Noble. She described meeting Joseph Smith. "This was the first time I ever beheld a prophet of the

Lord, and I can truly say at the first sight that I had a testimony within my bosom that he was a man chosen of God to bring forth a great work in the last days." She later described a church meeting in Geneva, Ohio, where she heard Joseph preach. She said, "Never did I hear preaching sound so glorious to me as that did. I realized it was the truth of heaven, for I had a testimony of it myself."[10] That personal witness confirmed her initial impression.

A few years later, there was a great tumult in the Church in Kirtland. In this divided community, leaders who had once stood by Joseph became some of his greatest detractors. Some called for a new prophet in the same upper room of the Kirtland temple where they had witnessed the Spirit pour out in "copious effusion."[11] In her pragmatic and forthright manner, recent convert Desdemona Fullmer described her response to those who contended against Joseph: "Oliver Cowdery with others would say to me are you such a fool as still to go hear Joseph the fallen prophet. I said the Lord convinced me that he was a true prophet. And he has not told me that he is fallen yet."[12] Her own personal witness of Joseph's prophetic calling gave her the confidence to help her endure. Desdemona trusted God to speak to her; she expected that she would likewise know by revelation if she should change course. Moreover, Joseph trusted in the abundance of revelation to not only reinforce his role as prophet but to create a prophetic community. Distracting voices have only expanded over the years, with many clamoring for our attention, but the Lord's model still asks us to remember our own experience with the revelations of God and to trust the prophet's voice.

Such trust is not the same as blind obedience. Years later, Brigham Young expressed his fear of such unthinking obedience—that people might just assume a prophet is called of God rather than seeking to know for themselves. He said,

> I am more afraid that this people have so much confidence in their leaders that they will not inquire for themselves of God whether they are led by Him. I am fearful they settle down in a state of blind self-security trusting their eternal destiny in the hands of their leaders with a reckless confidence that in itself would thwart the purposes of God in their salvation, and weaken what influence they could give their leaders, did they know for themselves, by the revelations of Jesus, that they are led the right way. Let every man and woman know, by the whisperings of the Spirit of God to themselves, whether their leaders are walking in the path the Lord dictates or not.[13]

For Brigham, one's personal communication with God was foundational. With a witness from God, we can trust those called by God and offer our support.

From the first day of the Church, the Lord emphasized our need for a prophet as a mouthpiece for the Lord while acknowledging the "patience and faith" that trusting in a fallible mortal to be God's servant requires. As President Harold B. Lee said, "There will be some things that take patience and faith."[14] Perhaps the prophet says something in an unexpected timeline, perhaps the prophet stays silent on a change we were hoping for, perhaps the prophet's words cause significant reflection and lead us to change our behavior. What is the point of a prophet who always tells us what we expect or who only ever bolsters our insistence that we are in the right? Just as we wait "patiently on the Lord," the prophetic promises come in a timeline the Lord chooses, not our own. It requires our faith to trust in the prophet and to know how to apply those directions to ourselves.

5

The Tyranny of a Burning Bosom

Section 9

In practice we often struggle to recognize the revelatory abundance available to us. As I grew up in the Church, I felt like 98.6 percent of the talks I heard on personal revelation used a single model of personal revelation that drew on the Lord's words to Oliver Cowdery from April 1829; what we know as section 9. I understood this as *the* model of revelation. Firstly, "study it out in your mind," and then "ask me if it be right," in which case "your bosom" would "burn within you" (9:8). Perhaps we like section 9 because it seems like an easy formula: check off the boxes and get your desired result. There was just one problem—I'd never felt something I would describe as a burning in my bosom. Isn't burning uncomfortable? I didn't know what to do with that.

Moreover, the only other option for a revelatory response I saw in this model was a stupor of thought—an absence of an answer. There were times when I thought I might have felt a direct "no" from the Lord. There were other times when I felt a "yes!" or a nudge, nudge, "this way" or a "wait, be patient."

In other words, my experience didn't match up with what I thought was *the* pattern of personal revelation from scripture. In this chapter, we will use section 9 to consider the danger of a single revelation model and explore what we miss when we assume that God only communicates in one way.

The Problem of a Single Pattern

Contrary to inclinations of a singular one-size-fits-all formula, Elder Richard Scott quells any wistful thinking while strengthening our hope: "I am convinced that there is no simple formula or technique that would immediately allow you to master the ability to be guided by the voice of the Spirit. Our Father expects you to learn how to obtain that divine help by exercising faith in Him and His Holy Son, Jesus Christ."[1] God wants to communicate with us and has gifted us the skills to learn how to communicate with Him.

The Lord's preface suggests that one of the characteristics of God, one of the facets of God's omnipotence and God's continued desire to communicate, is an ability to ever tailor the message to the audience, which is us. "Behold, I am God and have spoken it; these commandments are of me, and were given unto my servants in their weakness, after the manner of their language, that they might come to understanding" (1:24). God understands the weakness of us, "his servants," and of all humanity. God created us and placed us in mortality. And God wants to communicate with us in a manner that we will understand, despite our human limitations. This is foundational to a theology of revelatory abundance.

Today, I think that the pattern outlined in section 9 *can* be useful—maybe pro and con lists are your favorite way to "study it out in your mind" when you're trying to receive revelation and make a decision. I have had times when I planned to do something, but it consistently disappeared from my mind and my to-do-list until the opportunity passed. Perhaps that was a "stupor of thought." Maybe the lack of an answer was the response. The steps in section 9 can be *a* pattern, but they should never be considered the *only* pattern. There is never just one blueprint through which God speaks to us. The context of the oft-quoted section 9 was Oliver's attempt at translating the Book of Mormon, and while that does not nullify its application to broader contexts, it might temper it. Perhaps some of that revelatory direction was specific to the process of translation.

In those quiet moments when I seriously considered my own experience, I knew I had received communication from God. It just came differently for me. A "burning in the bosom" isn't my manner of language. When my experience didn't align with a scripture I understood as a singular pattern, I had to wrestle to understand how God communicated with *me*. Years later, I read Elder Dallin Oaks say that he wasn't sure if he had ever felt something he would label a "burning in the bosom." Having that possibility articulated brought relief I didn't know I needed. He said, "What does a 'burning in the bosom' mean? Does it need to be a feeling of caloric heat, like the burning produced by combustion? If that is the meaning, I have never had a burning in the bosom." Hearing this, I felt I wasn't alone anymore. He continued, "Surely, the word 'burning' in this scripture signifies a feeling of comfort and serenity. That is the witness many receive. That is the way revelation works."[2] For me, this expanded the possibility of recognizing revelation.

After Our Manner of Language

We saw in the Lord's preface that the Lord speaks to me in my "weakness" after my "manner ... of language" so that I "might come to understanding" (1:24). While we may instantly think of our laundry list of weaknesses that we want to fix, this is "weakness" singular. Not plural. We're all weak; it's our mortal condition. Some people's weaknesses are readily apparent; for others, they are hidden deep below, away from the world. But for all of us, weakness is our mortal state. And God still wants to communicate with us "in our weakness." We can all learn to hear and feel His seeking after us. God will speak to us "after our manner of language."

Our "manner of ... language" might be our native

tongue. God will not communicate to us in Japanese if our native tongue is Dagaare, nor in Quichean if we speak Danish. By extension, the Lord won't speak to us in a way that is unnatural or foreign to us. I have a friend who has heard an audible voice when God wants to communicate with her, but that is not generally how God communicates with me. Sometimes, God speaks to me in inaudible phrases—very often scriptural phrases that stick with me like they've been glued to my forehead on a particularly effective sticky note. Other times, it is through feelings: I feel God tell me, "Nope. Don't even think about it." In our premortal life we could communicate with God freely, but that is covered to our minds in the present. Passing through a veil of forgetfulness obfuscates our prior relationship with God and we need a lifetime to learn through our experience how God communicates with us individually.

Perhaps had I focused on the latter clause, "feel[ing] that it is right" (9:8), I could have earlier expanded my own sense of revelatory abundance. I might have recognized that talks I had heard, scriptures generally, and the Doctrine and Covenants specifically don't ever just offer a single model of revelation. Moreover, *all* individuals are not the same. Intuitively, we know that we are all born as different people, even before we are shaped by life's experiences. Yet, at times, we act as though everyone is built the same way and that the voice of God will speak in exactly the same way to all people. The tyranny of a single model can limit the condition of the revelatory possibility for each of us. A singular focus on one model to the exclusion of all others limits the possibility of learning how God speaks to each of us individually and negates the valuable experiences of others.

I know that not having a one-size-fits-all checklist for communicating with God can feel intimidating. If we ever become frustrated that we can't clearly hear God's voice, we should remember that this isn't simple for anyone. No one snaps their fingers and just gets it; we *all* have to learn the skill ourselves. That was the case for Elder Taiichi Aoba, who is a potter. Asked to teach a class at a youth conference, he drew upon his profession. He modeled how one would center the clay, and it looked easy—magically, he transformed clay blocks into works of art. He asked the youth if they wanted to attempt it, and they all wanted to try. The volunteers assumed it would be easy, yet very soon, clay was "flying around the room." They mistakenly assumed that it was as easy as he made it look, but he had honed his craft and his ability to center the clay and create beautiful objects over decades.[3] (I feel this quite poignantly, as I had to take a college pottery class a second time before I passed it. Centering the clay was my impatient self's nemesis.) He taught them about centering their lives in Christ; I also see this applying to revelation and any spiritual skill we need to learn. Learning about it in the abstract is never enough. We need practice to learn the skill.

Years ago, President James Faust compared the process of revelation to using an old-school crystal radio set. Long before we had digital tuners and podcasts that just needed a single tap to hear clearly, these finicky radios were the best technology available. He described the difficult process of getting a clear signal: you had to "find the right pinpoint, a little valley or peak on the crystal where the signal was received. Just a millimeter off on either side of that point and I would lose the signal and get scratchy static. Over time, with patience and perseverance, good eyesight, and a steady hand, I learned to find the signal point on the crystal without too much difficulty."[4] President Faust continued, "So it is with inspiration. We must attune ourselves to the inspiration from God and tune out the scratchy static. We must work at being tuned in. Most of us need a long time to become tuned in."[5] And unlike a crystal radio or a pottery wheel that basically works the same way for all, revelation works a little differently for each of us. We have to learn how to tune ourselves or center ourselves to individually hear the voice of the Lord.

Eliza R. Snow grew up in Mentor, Ohio, not far from Kirtland. Eliza came from a family of seekers and learned to seek religious truth in her youth. In the early 1830s, her family learned of Joseph Smith and the Church of Christ, and her mother and sister quickly joined the Church. Eliza met Joseph Smith and liked him but thought he might be *too* charismatic and the restoration he promised just a "flash in the pan." She wrote, "It was just what my soul had hungered for, but I thought it was a hoax." She studied scripture for four years, trying to decide what to do. In the spring of 1835, her mother and sister returned from Kirtland abuzz from their experience there and "reported of the faith and humility of those who had received the gospel as taught by Joseph—the progress of the work, the order or the organization of the priesthood, and the frequent manifestations of the power of God." "The spirit bore witness to [her] of the truth," though Eliza worried that she "had waited already a little too long." Maybe she could have decided to be baptized earlier, but maybe her seeking was just on her own timeline. Whatever the case, she was now certain that God wanted her to be baptized, and she was determined to follow God; she wrote that "her heart [was] fixed." The time helped her be certain, and she would not repent of her decision.[6]

For Eliza, scripture and the witness of others were critical to her experience. We all have a different manner of language. Sometimes the Lord communicated with Joseph Smith through objects that became connected with the Book of Mormon translation as well as other revelatory acts. Nephite interpreters were included in the stone box with the gold plates. Joseph found his first seer stone years before he had the plates or considered translating them himself. While the idea of revelation-inviting objects may seem foreign to our own current circumstances, such objects were a part of Joseph Smith's world and religious context. In the American Northeast in the 1820s, "treasure-seeking was part of an attempt to recapture the simplicity and magical power associated with apostolic Christianity."[7] The Lord used a medium that was familiar to Joseph and helped him to understand what his gifts were. His gifts of the Spirit were never about finding buried treasure, despite his family's indigent circumstances. Rather, the Lord spoke to Joseph in a manner he would understand.

In the portion of his letter from Liberty Jail that is now

canonized in the Doctrine and Covenants, Joseph Smith calls that gift of the Holy Ghost "the unspeakable gift ... not revealed since the world was until now" (121:26). Here Joseph is channeling Pauline language to describe the gift of the Holy Ghost. If that gift is indescribable, then might revelation that comes via the Holy Ghost also be difficult to verbalize? After Joseph's first experience with revelatory abundance, he struggled to find words capable of describing his experience—we already mentioned his continuing debate over whether fire or light best characterized the glory of God. Even the most eloquent among us at times struggles to put words to the transcendent and ineffable, yet God promises to communicate with us in a manner we can grasp. Moreover, we never know exactly what another is feeling. We might recognize some external sign when another person has been moved by the Spirit, but we can't say with precision what they are experiencing—they themselves might struggle with an accurate description. Understanding how God speaks to us is not something that anyone else can do for us. We must learn by experience.

If the Lord speaks to us in a manner that is tailored to us—"after our manner of language"—it opens up the possibilities for adaptation as well as recognizes commonalities that we can share. Maybe "a burning in the bosom" works for many people, just not me. I personally feel the Spirit in a variety of ways: sometimes the Spirit makes me confident, sometimes it makes me feel hyper and ready to act, other times it provides an overwhelming peace. I'm a big fan of Joseph's description of "pure intelligence flowing" unto me.

FIGURE 5.1. Common Themes in How Students Experience Revelation.

But when it comes to big questions in my life, they tend to follow a pattern I have learned over the years. As I teach and talk with my students about revelation, I ask them to think about how they receive revelation. Over several years, I kept track of students' responses, which I've formed here into a word cloud. Of course, we see a number of commonalities, general principles that work for various people, like peace or an absence of anxiety. But there are many other unique responses, such as feeling "like warm pjs just out of the dryer," "feeling a kick in the shins," or a "cleverly candid" response. These might be different descriptions of similar feelings, but each individual offers a distinct semantic explanation. How does one "feel that it is right"?

As we continue to gain this skill, we learn which patterns the Lord uses to communicate with us collectively, which might work with our experience, and how we "feel that it is right" individually. No one else can perfectly tell me how this works—just like no one can perfectly tell you how this works. We each have to work to develop that skill. Do you know the Lord's pattern of communicating with you?

6

Growing into the Spirit of Revelation

Sections 6 and 8

When Moroni first appeared to Joseph, he quoted the prophecies of Joel 2 and promised they were about to be fulfilled. "I will pour out my spirit upon all flesh; and your sons and your daughters shall prophesy" (Joel 2:28). For me, it is comforting to know that this time of revelatory abundance was prophesied. That's wonderful news. But it still takes a lifetime of practice and dedication to hear the voice of God. When we choose to listen, we can "grow into the principle of revelation."[1] Relief Society General President Julie Beck argued, "The ability to qualify for, receive, and act on personal revelation is the single most important skill that can be acquired in this life."[2] Rarely can we speak in such absolute terms and not be dreadfully wrong or at least a little oblivious. Yet the revelatory abundance established in the revelations of the Doctrine and Covenants suggests just that; receiving personal revelation is a skill. Speaking the language of heaven might have come naturally in our prior life, yet in the wilderness of mortality, we need to relearn how to hear the voice of the Lord.

In the last chapter, we considered God's ability to tailor the message to us and how we might recognize it. Despite the absence of a single formula, we all have the opportunity to learn the skill of revelation throughout our lives. This chapter will explore the process of what Joseph called "grow[ing] into the spirit of revelation."[3] President Nelson has likewise recently reminded us of this principle and urged us to learn how the Spirit speaks to us: "to grow into" it.[4] If we listen carefully, we might hear the voice of God. If we consider revelation a skill learned over a lifetime, we can value all growth, no matter how small. Learning the process is primary.

Growing Methods

In the summer of 1839, Joseph Smith gave a discourse to the Twelve as they gathered in Commerce, Illinois, before they were to leave on a mission to Great Britain. Wilford Woodruff wrote notes as Joseph spoke on various topics, including "the spirit of revelation":

> A person may profit by noticeing the first intimations of the spirit of revelation for Instance when you feel pure

intelligence flowing unto you it may give you sudden stoks [strokes] of Ideas that by noticing it you may find it fulfilled the same day or soon ie those things that were presented unto your mind by the spirit of God will come to pass & thus by learning the Spirit of God & understanding it you may grow into the principle of Revelation untill you become perfe[c]ted in Christ Jesus.[5]

Perhaps Joseph's description of "intelligence flowing" or "sudden strokes of ideas" works with our experience, yet it is still a process. God doesn't just suddenly open our heads and install a permanent conduit to heaven to provide a continual surge of divine information. We learn bit by bit, piece by piece. We notice something. We notice something more. Conversation by conversation. Understanding takes time and work to hone the skill to hear and understand God for ourselves. The Doctrine and Covenants documents some of the processes that Joseph and other early Saints went through—asking questions with faith, wrestling, getting answers (or not getting them), wrestling some more, and moving forward. It was a process for them to learn how to hear the voice of the Lord, and it is a process for each of us. We must each build a relationship with God through this kind of intellectual and spiritual work.

While we've already begun to unpack specific pieces of the following verses from the Lord's preface to the revelations (section 1), when we consider them all together, we get a powerful and succinct description of the plan of salvation. Perhaps we can think of it as a proposal of the process of our mortal experience and the role of God's revelations:

> Behold, I am God and have spoken it; these commandments are of me, and were given unto my servants in their weakness, after the manner of their language, that they might come to understanding. And inasmuch as they erred it might be made known; And inasmuch as they sought wisdom they might be instructed; And inasmuch as they sinned they might be chastened, that they might repent; And inasmuch as they were humble they might be made strong, and blessed from on high, and receive knowledge from time to time. (1:24–28)

These verses suggest a process of how we "grow into the principle of revelation." We learn, we mess up, we seek wisdom, we learn, we sin, we repent, and if we continue to humbly petition heaven, our mortal weakness "might be made strong" through divine blessings and knowledge. Note the distinction suggested between mistakes and sins. They are not the same, but both are a part of our mortal experience. None of us escapes either. We learn over time, bit by bit, "line upon line, precept upon precept, here a little and there a little" (2 Nephi 28:30; Doctrine and Covenants 98:12, 128:21; cf. Isaiah 28:10). The elemental character of divine knowledge is incremental. As transcendentalist Henry David Thoreau, Joseph Smith's contemporary, quipped, "knowledge does not come to us in details, but in flashes of light from heaven."[6]

Learning by Experience

The revelations collected in the Doctrine and Covenants practically walk Joseph and other servants of God through

IMAGE 3: "Great Elm" on Dairy Hill (ca. 1911–1913), by George Edward Anderson. Image courtesy of L. Tom Perry Special Collections, Harold B. Lee Library, Brigham Young University.

the individual process of learning to hear and act on the word of the Lord. And the revelations offer not a single model of how God works but a multitude of examples, an abundance. Rather than a narrow tyrannical model, we will consider the broader experience of Oliver Cowdery, for whom Joseph's revelations offered a practical theology of communication with God and began to shape the abundance of revelatory models offered to us through scripture. Though Oliver would falter and separate himself from the Saints for almost a decade, perhaps he even more clearly illustrates the process of growing in revelation: he made mistakes, he sinned, but he was not cut off forever; after a time, he remembered, he repented, and he returned.

Oliver first met the Smith family as he traveled to upstate New York to work as a teacher. He boarded with the Smiths in their Manchester home and learned of their son Joseph and his work. He asked God to "know concerning the truth of [those] things" (6:22). Oliver had already learned the necessity of asking God. The first major theme of the revelatory instructions he received was about asking: "If you will ask of me you shall receive; if you will knock it shall be opened to you" (6:5). The Lord later reminded Oliver that "blessed art thou" for learning to ask God, and "as often as thou hast inquired thou hast received the instruction of my Spirit" (6:14). The Lord pleads with Oliver to continue to ask, and to do so with a particular mindset: "ask in faith, with an honest heart, believing that you shall receive" (8:1, also reiterated in 10). Moreover, shortly thereafter, the Lord called him out when his first inclination was not to call on God. "You took no thought save it was to ask me" (9:7).

That Spirit led him to travel nearly 300 miles to meet Joseph Smith and ultimately changed the course of his whole life. He arrived, and they began to work on the Book of Mormon translation, yet his questions did not suddenly cease. Part of God's response was to turn him back to remember how God had spoken to him earlier. "Did I not speak peace to your mind concerning the matter? What greater witness can you have than from God?" (6:23). There are a couple of clues in this verse that teach us how to recognize when God is speaking. First, peace becomes a priority marker when we're trying to hear the voice of the Lord. It is one of those shared modes of revelation. God endeavored to "speak peace" to Oliver to confirm the truth of the revelation. Second, remembering how God has spoken to us in the past is central to understanding God's will in the present. Elder Neal A. Maxwell was fond of saying, "The Holy Ghost will often preach sermons to us from the pulpit of memory."[7] Sometimes, a weighty sermon comes in the flash of a memory or a few words from scripture. Remembering how God has blessed us in the past thus plays a central role in helping us to receive and understand God's word in the present.

When the Book of Mormon manuscript pages were stolen, Joseph was bereft. The Lord called on him to remember a larger principle, "Remember, remember that it is not the work of God that is frustrated, but the work of men" (3:3). The Lord told Joseph he had "feared man more than God" and clearly reproved Joseph's sin (3:7). Being a prophet who had received many revelations did not make him immune from sin: "if thou art not aware thou wilt fall" (7:9).

But immediately the Lord urged him to remember another important principle: that "God is merciful" (3:10). Through the revelations, the Lord pled with the Saints to remember a number of important principles that could be particularly illuminating considering their immediate context: "remember the worth of souls," "remember [God's] words," "remember faith," "remember the poor," and many more.[8] In other ways, the Lord can use the Spirit's pricking of our memories to remind us of principles we have momentarily forgotten.

Returning to Oliver, remembering was not only a momentary need for Oliver. It was a crucial necessity for him and for the rest of us. He needed to remember not only God's words but also His gifts. The latter part of section 8 considers a peculiar and specific gift given to Oliver. The text of the revelation originally read, "the gift of working with the sprout; behold it has told you many things" (8:6). This referred to dousing, or the gift of using a divining rod. Today, some farmers still find water using divining rods. While teaching at BYU-Idaho, every semester, I had at least one student who knew someone with that gift ready to help someone else find a water source on their property.

While the specificity of the original revelation testifies to the individuality of the message to Oliver, over time, the revelation was edited so that it might be understood not just by Oliver but by any reader of the text. What originally read the "gift of working with the sprout" was changed by Sidney Rigdon to read the "gift of working with the rod" for publication in the *Book of Commandments*. This change from a "sprout"—a sprouted branch, a more colloquial name for a Y-shaped divining stick—to a "rod" implicitly referenced Numbers 17:8. That's when Aaron's rod suddenly and miraculously sprouted blossoms and then almonds. An extremely biblically literate audience knew Aaron's rod was the means by which Moses performed miracles.[9]

In a later edit for the next edition, the 1835 Doctrine and Covenants, they changed "rod" to the "gift of Aaron." Now the allusion was explicit and accessible to a much wider audience. Moreover, the revelation clearly compared Oliver to Aaron, just as the Lord had compared Joseph to Moses. Just as Moses was "slow of speech" and Aaron could "speak well" (Exodus 4:10, 14), Oliver likewise had more communication skills and education than did Joseph. It would take years for Joseph to come into his own gifts of speaking and preaching. As historian Steve Harper maintains, "Far from discouraging Oliver from using his revelatory gifts, the revelation teaches him how to use them legitimately. The Lord legitimized, not criticized, these gifts."[10] The editing process may have obscured the specific means by which Oliver participated in miraculous events, the divining rod, but it highlighted the divine gifts that Oliver possessed, his position, and how he might further "seek to bring forth the cause of Zion" (6:6). With the change the very personal revelation offered to Oliver was now intelligible and applicable to a broader audience.

Oliver had learned the value of asking; asking will remain a perpetual need. The Lord had reminded Oliver of the importance of remembering principles already learned and answers already given. In section 8, the Lord offered another model of revelation: "I will tell you in your mind and in your heart, by the Holy Ghost, which shall come upon you and which shall dwell in your heart" (8:2). Neither our intellect nor our emotion is sufficient on its own to enable divine communication. We need both to hear the voice of God.

The general context of section 8 to Oliver only heightens our understanding of the importance of this model. In the nineteenth century, the ideas of the head and the heart were divided on a strict gender binary for many. Some thought the head represented male intellectual traits. On the other hand, a caricature of women depicted them oppositionally as emotive, unserious beings represented by the heart. While anciently the heart represented the cosmic center of a person, in the post-enlightenment period, the heart could be maligned as the provenance of silly, flighty women. Yet, the model the voice of the Lord calls "*the* spirit of revelation" does not privilege either side of an assumed binary over another. There is no binary at all, in fact: "I will tell you in your mind and in your heart." All people need to use intellect as well as emotions to hear God's voice. Then-Elder Jeffrey Holland called it both "a reasonable way and a revelatory way."[11] These two witnesses of a revelation can help us guard against deception.

The Spirit of Revelation

The Lord continues, declaring, "Now, behold, this is the spirit of revelation; behold, this is the spirit by which Moses brought the children of Israel through the Red Sea on dry ground." The Lord's chosen instructive example of the "spirit of revelation" is Moses parting the Red Sea (8:3). Why would that be *the* example? Are we suddenly going back to a single model? If we highlight this moment in Exodus, we generally focus on its miraculous properties, yet here in modern revelation, the Lord's voice insists the "dry ground" upon which the children of Israel walked was not just miraculous but modeled "the spirit of revelation" (8:3).

Let's consider some of the abundant ways that this scriptural event might model the principle of revelation. Firstly, Moses was in need. With an expanse of water ahead, the children of Israel looked up and saw the Egyptians quickly approaching. These were not casual questions being asked by Moses or his people; they needed help quickly, and the people collectively called out for God. The people remembered their past experiences with the Egyptians and understandably "were sore afraid." Their fear led them to begin to doubt Moses and to question the miracles that had gotten them to that place (Exodus 14:10–12). Though Moses likewise called out to the Lord for assistance, in contrast to his people, he did not remember Egypt in fear; he remembered his relationship with the Lord that developed during that time. He had heard and acted on the Lord's words numerous times before. He then called out to his people, "Fear ye not, stand still, and see the salvation of the Lord which he will shew you to day" (Exodus 14:13). A second essential lesson here is that rather than taking counsel from fear, as did his people, Moses held on to the faith he had in his relationship with God, knowing God would fight for them. And his people could trust in their prophet as a worthy representative of the Lord.

The Lord told them to stop talking and to act out in faith. The third point was their need to trust God and "go forward." He placed the cloud, the *shekinah*—the visible sign of His presence—between them and the Egyptians, giving them the cover and the light they needed to pack up and move ahead. And when they went forward, they did so "on dry ground through the midst of the sea" (Exodus 14:16). As Elder Holland considered this moment in his remarkable talk "Cast Not Away Therefore Your Confidence," he reminded us, "Nobody had ever crossed the Red Sea this way, but so what? There's always a first time. With the spirit of revelation, dismiss your fears and wade in with both feet."[12] If God directs it, God will provide the way.

So perhaps rather than a narrow example better suited to a very specific instance, this sweeping model provided by the children of Israel crossing the Red Sea can expand how we think of revelation—with an abundance of possibilities. We learn that the animating principle of revelation is action—revelation is not static. As Elder Holland detailed, in the "process of revelation and in making important decisions, fear almost always plays a destructive, sometimes paralyzing role."[13] We need not denigrate ourselves for fearing; it is a part of our mortal condition. But what we do with that fear matters. God is worthy of our trust. We can confide in His words. Look up and go forward. God's word is sure.

For many of us, life provides moments where we can

choose to faithfully trust in God's revelation, even if those moments are not as dramatic as the parting of the Red Sea. Let's consider the example of Mary Fielding. By 1836, when sisters Mary and Mercy Fielding were baptized in Toronto, Canada, along with their brother Joseph, the sisters were in their mid-thirties—confirmed spinsters by nineteenth-century standards. They gathered to Kirtland; unexpectedly, Mercy soon married, and she and her new husband were quickly called on a mission back to Canada. Joseph was then called on a mission to their family of origin in England, and Mary was left alone in Kirtland. Like many unmarried educated women in the nineteenth century and many a good Austen or Brontë heroine, she tried to provide for herself as a governess.

In the fall of 1837, she wrote a lengthy letter to her sister detailing the chaos growing around her. She had been in an acceptable position for a time, but it was ending, and she didn't yet have a new job. Her personal life was feeling a little chaotic and she was also surrounded by the collective chaos of apostasy in the fall of 1837. She looked to scripture, and she looked to God. Though the next day she would be "at liberty or without imployment," Mary told her sister she felt "my mind pretty much at rest on that subject. I have called upon the Lord for direction and trust he will open my way."[14] She was not entirely without fear or worries, but most of the time, she could ignore them and focus on her faith. Her mind was mostly at peace. God's answer might take time, but she knew it would come. Regarding the widespread religious exodus from the Church, she maintained her faith that "the Lord will support us and give us grace and strength for the day if we continue to put our trust in Him and devote ourselves unreservedly to His service." Mary maintained peace "pretty much" despite the turmoil surrounding her because of her relationship with God. She asked in faith and trusted the answers would come.[15]

Despite the absence of a perfect one-size-fits-all formula for revelation or instantaneous mastery of the process, we all have the opportunity to grow into revelation in mortality. God speaks, and we each can choose to learn how to hear it. We can choose not to be paralyzed by our fears. We can always listen to the Lord and build our faith rather than feeding our fear. As Moses did with his people, prophets can see beyond our immediate bubble, correcting our myopia or near-sightedness.[16] We can benefit from their relationship with God as we build our own. Once we understand the word of God to us, then we must trust it and move forward, knowing that God will provide a way.

7

Cautionary Tales

Sections 50, 51, 52, 54, 58, 60, 64

"Wherefore," the revelation declares, "be not deceived, but continue in steadfastness" (50:2). There are warnings of all shapes and sizes woven throughout the revelatory texts of the Doctrine and Covenants. These warnings try to help us take "the Holy Spirit for [our] guide," "beware lest ye are deceived," and avoid those things that could cause us to "stumble and fall," change the direction of our path, or injure us.[1] Beginning with the Lord's preface, we learn that one of the modes of God's voice is this "voice of warning" (1:4). I could argue that the theme of avoiding deception is nearly as prevalent as that of revelatory abundance, particularly in the first half of the revelations; we've already seen several warnings from the Lord in the revelations we've

95

considered. Is all this concern warranted? How do we receive such caveats? Do we see God as a helicopter parent who excessively warns and hovers at arm's length or a parent who warns, teaches, and then steps away to let us learn? What follows is certainly not comprehensive, but we will consider a smattering of different stumbling blocks that can easily hamper our ability to hear the Lord's voice clearly. Using the Kirtland revelations of 1831 as a foundation, in this chapter, we point out a number of cautions from the Lord that commonly surface amidst our mortal journey, particularly as we "grow into revelation."

The Lord tells us in section 50 that there are "many false spirits which have gone forth in the earth, deceiving the world" (50:2). A false spirit? Nefarious ghosts? Fiendish devils? For a moment, let's return to our earlier discussion of how God commands us to ask (chapter 2) to think about "false spirits." Part of the rationale of a command to "in all things ... ask of God" was "that ye may not be seduced by evil spirits, or doctrines of devils, or the commandments of men; for some are of men, and others of devils" (46:7). These potential deceptions take many forms. Some could be abstract ideas that lead us away from God. Others might be real beings—some benign but misguided, others intent on destroying us. Perhaps Satan wants to push us off course; perhaps we latch onto a destructive idea, or perhaps it is just a well-meaning individual who doesn't know what God has revealed to us. Whatever the mode of the false spirits, we all need help to discern them to avoid this pitfall.

When Joseph went to the grove to pray out loud for

the first time, he described it as a "fruitless attempt," not from lack of desire but from something more sinister. He recalled, "my tongue seemed to be swollen in my mouth so that I could not utter." He tried to pray "but could not."[2] In another account of the vision, he described being "seized upon by some power which entirely overcame" him and bound his tongue (Joseph Smith—History 1:15–16). After his First Vision, Joseph said a minister dismissed him "with great contempt, saying it was all of the devil" and "that there were no such things as visions or revelations in these days" (JSH 1:21). These two moments—one anticipatory to his miraculous vision and one in the aftermath—might tell us something about the range of false spirits. Before, it seemed that there was an evil spirit, perhaps *the* evil spirit, who "doomed [Joseph] to sudden destruction" and rather dramatically tried to stop his prayer from ever leaving his mouth in this crucial moment. What if Joseph hadn't endured and "exert[ed] all [his] powers to call upon God to deliver" him? (Joseph Smith—History 1:16). And then the misguided minister, repeating a particular Protestant concern about the chaos of visions and the authority of the Bible, tried to negate what Joseph had experienced, or at least to stop him from talking about it. What if Joseph had listened and discounted his own experience in favor of another's limited vision? In this chapter, we will use the early Kirtland revelations to consider those impediments that can block our ability to hear the voice of God: Can we ignore, avoid, or at least limit those things trying to block our way?

Judging New and Strange Ways

In the fall of 1830, there was a huge influx of new members to the struggling Church of Christ. As the first group of missionaries officially sent out by the Lord traveled to their destination, they stopped in Kirtland almost incidentally and very quickly baptized more than one hundred people. The missionaries' break lasted longer than they intended, but after two weeks, they were on their way again, leaving the new converts to fend for themselves with insufficient Books of Mormon to spread around. For months, these new converts negotiated their newfound faith alone. Like the earliest Christians, many of them listened to new scripture in community. In the following months, some interesting practices crept in: they acted out the Book of Mormon story, received "visions and revelations," and engaged in many other enthusiastic and charismatic displays. When Church leaders began to visit Kirtland months later, most did not find these practices "edifying" or "congenial to the doctrine and spirit of the gospel."[3] These Church leaders questioned the orthodoxy of the "new and strange ways," but not wanting to "err in judgment," waited to consult with Joseph.[4] This likewise coincided with the Mrs. Hubble moment we discussed in chapter 4.

These early Kirtland revelations demonstrate Joseph's prophetic action—a multi-prong revelatory effort to correct the Saints. He asked the Lord to help them distinguish what was true and false. He received new revelations, attempting to quell bad ideas by supplanting them with good ones (42). The Lord called out the "false spirits" as "abominations." It's important to note that the people were not abominations for falling to these false spirits; the people were learning to distinguish. They could change—if they "were faithful and endure[d]" they would "inherit eternal life" (50:2–5). Joseph worked with the Saints to correct the errors in the ensuing months. He further organized the Church, tried to help the Saints coming from New York, and continued to call missionaries to spread the message of the Restoration (sections 46–52).

In May, the revelation in section 50 specifically addressed the false spirits. The first warning made in the revelation was about hypocrites. Hypocrite comes from the Greek word *hypokritēs* and literally points to an actor, someone playing a role. There will always be those who are acting a part, not revealing their true selves or their true motives, and they can be damaging and destructive to us. We all need to be on guard. The Lord promises that these people will ultimately be detected and "brought to judgment" but offers no assurance as to the timeline: "either in life or death, even as I will" (50:8). In the cautions that follow, the Lord references the Spirit as the ultimate detector to protect us from disingenuous and feigning people and other forms of "false spirits."

Moreover, as the revelation continues, the Lord placed great value on "reason[ing] together," echoing language from Isaiah. He calls out, "come ... let us reason together, that [we] may understand. Let us reason even as [one] reasoneth with another face to face" (50:10–11). For the Lord, reason and the Spirit are not opposites but elements that work hand in hand to lead us to understanding. Both are gifts from God.

The elements of this model to detect deception might challenge some of our preconceived notions. Why would we want to talk to, much less reason with, someone who might be led by a false spirit? Why would we want to be in the same room with them? And how does reason work with the Spirit rather than against it? Perhaps our initial discomfort is because it is a new idea to us; perhaps it is a cultural practice that feels foreign to us; our initial impressions are not *always* right, and sometimes we need to take that time to "reason together" and see what the Spirit tells us.

The revelation tells us that the way to both preach and receive "the word of truth" is "by the Comforter, in the spirit of truth" (50:17). The reasonable conversation enables both participants, she "that preacheth" and she "that receiveth," to "understand one another, and both are edified and rejoice together" (50:22). As President Russell Nelson quipped, "good inspiration is based on good information."[5]

In more than one instance, early Saints used the models presented in section 50 to determine whether spirits were true or false.[6] Do we preach and receive the word of God "by the Spirit of truth or by some other way"? Does it edify? Does it build us up? Does it add to those things that we've already identified as truth? Moreover, section 50 testifies to the layering quality of truth. Light and truth come from God, and they build on each other. When we "receive light, and continueth in God," we receive more light, growing "brighter and brighter until the perfect day" (50:17–25).

The revelation ends with a reminder that though the day will come when all comes together, that time is not yet, but all is in God's hands. Be patient and "watch, therefore, that ye may be ready" (50:41–46).

Finding Our Own Track

The following month, June 1831, the Lord gave another caution to help us avoid deception. This pattern included three practical behaviors: praying, having a contrite spirit, and obeying the Lord's ordinances (52:15–16). It seems that a desire to communicate with God, be repentant, and remain faithful can become a solid foundation to avoid deception. Ordinances can have a multi-valent meaning, pointing to both the covenants we make with God and the commandments God asks us to obey. The Lord is willing to take our limited offering and transform it into something strong, promising that we "shall bring forth fruits of praise and wisdom" (52:17). Elder Dale Renlund reminds us, "To evaluate metaphorical fruit, one needs to observe and discern whether it is good or not ... the Savior asks us to discern truth by observation and reasoning."[7]

After providing us with the pattern outlined above, the Lord then called a long list of elders as missionaries, expecting them to put the pattern into practice. They received this instruction: "Let all these take their journey unto one place, in their several courses, and one man should not build upon another's foundation, neither journey in another's track" (52:33). In both missions and mortality part of the challenge is finding our own path. We're not wholly alone, however. Remember the two lines of communication we discussed in chapter 4? Where the early missionaries were concerned, the Prophet offered general direction, and they needed to interpret what that meant for them. They needed to decide if they'd go right or left, ride in a carriage or walk, and what towns and villages they would pass through. Even if our destination is the same, we all need our own path.

To help us, we not only have the Prophet, we also have our faith community. Another element of seeking God's will is that we ask questions and receive answers to those questions in the company of others. This could be supportive and illuminating or potentially hazardous, as our community can hinder or expand our revelatory possibilities in a number of different ways. Sometimes, we just choose the path of least resistance—a well-worn path because it is easy, and others encourage us to do the same thing they've done. Sometimes, well-intentioned individuals, those who don't know God's will concerning us, get in the way. Speaking to a BYU Women's Conference, then-Elder Russell Ballard commented,

> Each of you must come to know what the Lord wants for you individually, given the choices before you.... Once you know the Lord's will, you can then move forward in faith to fulfill your individual purpose. One sister may be inspired to continue her education and attend medical school, allowing her to have a significant impact on her patients and to advance medical research. For another sister, inspiration may lead her to forgo a scholarship to a prestigious institution and instead begin a family much earlier than has

become common in this generation, allowing her to make a significant and eternal impact on her children now.

He continued,

> Is it possible for two similarly faithful women to receive such different responses to the same basic questions? Absolutely! What's right for one woman may not be right for another. That's why it is so important that we should not question each other's choices or the inspiration behind them.[8]

Do we want to help others fulfill God's will for them or be a hindrance to them? Elder Ballard continued addressing how we knowingly or unknowingly can become impediments for others as he instructed, "We should refrain from asking hurtful and unsupportive questions like 'Why are you going on a mission?' or 'Why aren't you on a mission?' or 'Why aren't you married?' or 'Why don't you have children?' We can all be kinder and more thoughtful of the situations in which our sisters throughout the world find themselves as they seek to follow the will of our Heavenly Father in their individual lives."[9] None of us needs more stumbling blocks. And if we are to create a Zion community where everyone can thrive, we don't want to become a stumbling block for others.

In like manner, there are times when cultural ideals and expectations don't offer room for the answer we receive. There are times when God's answer comes so out of the blue that it is difficult for us to receive it. Maybe we'll tread the same path as our parents or our ancestors, or maybe we'll blaze new trails. Whatever path we take, we need to know what God wants to communicate to us. Consider Karen Davidson's heartfelt desire to be a friend who "touches" the lives of others for good, one who "reflects" the Lord's "great mercy."[10] Our task is to open ourselves up to the possibility and extend the same grace to others.

Equal Considerations

In our desire to learn and accept the will of God, there are other potential stumbling blocks in our way. The Lord specifically labels temporal inequality as one of those impediments to receiving the "abundance of the manifestations of the Spirit." And even "grudging" temporal equality could withhold the abundance (70:13–14). The principles of the law of consecration were set up by the Lord to create an environment in which each individual specifically and the community generally could thrive both spiritually and temporally. As the Lord continued to build on "the Law" as established by section 42 of the Doctrine and Covenants, the Saints were instructed to "appoint" those "portions" which everyone needed to be "equal according to [their] circumstances and wants and needs" (51:3). This equality is not defined by sameness, but by creating an atmosphere in which all have what will enable them to thrive. We usually consider the temporal aspects of the Law, but the temporal is never divorced from the spiritual (29:34). In fact, the temporal practices we engage in now may well be preparation for eternity. Joseph's vision, recorded in section 76, introduced the idea that those who inherit celestial glory will be "equal in power, and in might, and in dominion" (76:95). Shortly thereafter, the Lord instructed that if they wanted to be "equal in the bonds of heavenly things," then they needed to practice equality in earthly things (78:5–6). Might a divine vision of equality create a place where everyone can thrive according to their "circumstances and ... wants and needs" with God's direction? Can we create a community where each individual can receive God's direction unencumbered by limitations?

Jane Smith's poverty could have been a hindrance to acting on the inspiration of God. She worked in a factory in Dundee, Scotland, making lace by hand, but despite her skill she did not have any money for her own "Easter bonnets and fine clothes and spring suits." Every extra pence went to their family immigration fund. They hoped to gather with the Saints in Utah. At church, girls of more financial means made fun of Jane's plain clothing; she would even take the long way home to avoid these girls. Baptized in her "thirteenth year," she remembered a testimony meeting when she felt "forcibly constrained" by the Spirit to get up and testify "to the truth." She could have let her youth, her inexperience, or her plain clothing stop her from contributing her witness, but she had received her own testimony and she "had to get up and bear testimony that Joseph Smith was a prophet of God." She would not let inequality amongst the Saints stop her from responding to the Spirit.[11]

Not Everything Matters

In August of 1830, as Joseph prepared the sacrament, he received a revelation where the Lord suggested the larger symbolism of the Lord's Supper was the most important element of the ritual; there was no need to quibble over the specific food used: "it mattereth not what ye shall eat or what ye shall drink" (27:2). All things are not of equal value nor equal importance. As we seek a closer relationship with God, sometimes we need help to determine what is most important. In this instance, the ordinance and the focus on the Savior were primary: if Joseph's eye was "single to my glory," then whether it was rice crackers, sprouted wheat rolls, or a smashed-up ball of white bread didn't really matter, at least spiritually. One with "an eye single to the glory of God" will still see distractions peripherally but will not lose focus on the Lord. The Lord helped Joseph determine what was most important.

Sometimes, we are hindered in our ability to receive and act upon revelation because we are paralyzed by an ideal that if we are in tune with the Lord, he will micromanage every detail of our decision-making. Not everything matters in the eternal scheme of things. Sometimes, the Lord is telling us to make a choice. It might be a moment to use our agency, to be "an agent unto" ourselves. (29:35) Maybe it doesn't matter if we're a doctor or a lawyer, a dog groomer or a coder. Maybe it doesn't matter if we buy a Honda or a Ford, wear Jordans or Sambas, or paint our house blue or green—we don't need "the personal assurance from the Spirit from daylight to dark on everything [we] do."[12] There are certainly times that our choices do matter, but if we've asked and are left without specific direction, then it's up to us to make a decision. Sometimes, we need the process of making the wrong decision to find the right one; sometimes, it isn't either/or, it's both/and (54:2, 8); sometimes, we are waffling between two good options, and the Lord is truly saying, "it mattereth not unto me" (62:5).

The next summer, a group of missionaries was to travel to the East, and they wanted direction from the Lord. Though they might have figured this out on their own, the Lord patiently revealed that the most important thing was that they "open[ed] their mouths" and preached along the way, but they could choose the mode of travel—"whether there be a craft made, or bought, as seemeth you good, it mattereth not unto me." They should decide and leave "speedily" (60:2, 5). They chose to travel by water and met some difficulties (including an unfortunate vision of the Destroyer), and they returned to ask the Lord for advice. The Lord's message to them did not entirely change but acknowledged He "suffered" or allowed the trial to happen because He wanted them to learn something. He was still concerned with their "haste," and He trusted them to decide the details of their journey: "it mattereth not unto me, after a little, if it so be that they fill their mission, whether they go by water or by land; let this be as it is made known unto them according to their judgments hereafter" (61:21–22).

Not long before this the Lord had tried to teach them "It is not meet that I should command in all things." The Lord suggests that if we want to be programmed and directed—"compelled in all things"—we can become slothful and unwise. The Lord trusts us, and as we develop a relationship with Him, we can draw upon His power to do good. The Lord wants us to be "anxiously engaged in a good cause and do many things of [our] own free will." We are not robots to be programmed but "agents unto [our]selves" (58:26–28). Sometimes we just need to act.

Timing

There is also the matter of the Lord's timing. One consistent message of the revelations is that the Lord's words are sure—"my words are sure and shall not fail. But," the Lord reminds us, "all things must come to pass in their time" (64:31–33). As we learn to receive abundant revelation, one impediment can be a failure to understand that the "reckoning of God's time" functions differently than our own (130:4–7). Learning to trust in the Lord requires complete confidence in God. In a remarkable devotional on "Timing," then-Elder Dallin Oaks counseled, "In all the important decisions in our lives, what is most important is to do the right thing. Second, and only slightly behind the first, is to do the right thing at the right time."[13] The right thing at the wrong time causes its own peculiar kind of agony. In those moments, our resolve to trust in the Lord is tested and tried, pulled and stretched. Similarly, Elder Neal A. Maxwell gently cautioned us, "When we are unduly impatient with an omniscient God's timing, we really are suggesting that we know what is best. Strange, isn't it—we who wear wristwatches seek to counsel Him who oversees cosmic clocks and calendars."[14] "Waiting patiently on the Lord" is sometimes the hardest thing the Lord asks of us, yet He promises that all those things that have afflicted us will "work together for [our] good" (98:2).

Part of giving our heart to the Lord, giving our whole selves and not holding anything back, is trusting in the Lord's timing. Elder Maxwell further suggested, "Since faith in the timing of the Lord may be tried, let us learn to say not only, 'Thy will be done,' but patiently also, 'Thy timing be done.'"[15] Remember the example of Mary Fielding Smith from chapter 6: when she was between jobs and facing financial hardship, as well as the turbulence caused by widespread apostasy in Kirtland, she kept the faith, knowing that an answer would come eventually. Will we be like her and wait patiently on the Lord? Even if it means facing uncertainty? Ultimately, the most important thing is the place of our heart. Do we desire to know God's will for us, His whole will, or do we only "desire to know the truth in part?" (49:2). Will we continue to want to hear God's voice and respond? President Henry Eyring said, "Part of the tragedy you must avoid is to discover too late that you missed an opportunity to prepare for a future only God could see for you."[16] Will we hear Him? In the Doctrine and Covenants hearing is never merely a mechanical operation of eardrums and sound waves, but a function of agency. We choose whether we want to hearken, whether we want to hear.

Hearkening might require that we move out of our comfort zones. President Uchtdorf commented on the impediment that our present comfort might become: "Brothers and sisters, as good as our previous experience may be, if we stop asking questions, stop thinking, stop pondering, we can thwart the revelations of the Spirit.... We can block the growth and knowledge our Heavenly Father intends for us. How often has the Holy Spirit tried to tell us something we needed to know but couldn't get past the massive iron gate of what we thought we already knew?"[17] Rather than attachment to what we thought was most important, "the spirit giveth life" and can animate our lives in ways we didn't think possible (2 Cor. 3:6).

This chapter offers cautions to help us avoid some of the stumbling blocks that might hinder our path to living in the Spirit and hearing Him—things that sometimes impede our way as we endeavor to "grow into revelation." But as we've discussed, revelation is never just a + b = c. Sometimes, easy answers are not forthcoming. There are times, despite all our efforts to move beyond the roadblocks to understand God's revelations, the heavens remain silent. The next chapter considers those moments when God stops speaking.

8

When Silence Reigns

Sections 98, 101, and 121

If revelation is abundant in the Restoration, then why are there times when we feel as though silence reigns? (38:12). At times, we cry out, "O God where are thou? And where is the pavilion that covereth thy hiding place?" (121:1–2). Even a half hour of "silence in heaven" in God's timeline can feel like an eternity to us (88:95). Even if it will eventually be "but a small moment," right now we may be asking, "O Lord, how long?" (121:7, 3).

Unexpectedly, when we've grown in revelation and are beginning to better understand how it is that God speaks to us individually, there will be times when the answers don't come, and the heavens are silent. In this chapter we will consider those times when we cannot fix it. Whatever the source, we can't find the answer to end the silence. These are the times when we call out, "Keep not thou silence, O God: hold not thy peace, and be not still, O God" (Psalm 83:1). Just as there is no one-size-fits-all formula to learning the process of revelation, there is no easy answer at such a time. Moreover, I am not sure that successfully navigating away the silence is always the goal.

In one of many injunctions throughout scripture to seek the Lord, Isaiah pleads with his people, "Seek ye the Lord while he may be found, call ye upon him when he is near." If He is near, take advantage of the moment. Forsake sin and repent when needed, for the Lord "will have mercy ... and abundantly pardon." The rationale for this, at least in part, seems to be because of our inability to always predict how God will act, for the Lord tells us, "My thoughts are not your thoughts, neither are your ways my ways" (Isaiah 55:6–8, echoed and reiterated in Doctrine and Covenants 88:62–3). For those who are actively seeking God's help, this unpredictability can wreak havoc on our souls and our sense of a relationship with God if we expect that God will always respond when we ask. Just as the revelations in the Doctrine and Covenants offer models for an abundance of revelation, there are likewise theological models for those times when answers are not forthcoming.

Firstly, sometimes the silence has a clinical source—anxiety or depression that block our way—and we are doing what we can. That requires significant patience on our part—patience with ourselves and patience with the Lord. Sometimes, the heavens fall silent because there is something that we need to change, and if we are honest with ourselves, we can change it. If we need to repent, repent. Are we willing to give away those sins that impede our way?

However, we are not always the problem. Sometimes, when the heavens feel shut to us, we incorrectly assume it is punishment even when we have faithfully sought to communicate with God and seek God's will. Those thoughts can only be destructive. Adam Miller encourages us to lean into the silence. He suggests, "You may discover that God's silence is not itself a rebuke but an invitation. The heavens aren't empty, they're quiet. And God, rather than turning you away, may be inviting you to share silence with him."[1]

Missouri's First Expulsion

In August 1833, before Joseph Smith began to hear of the tragedy of the Saints being expelled from Jackson County, Missouri, he received a revelation that possibly ignited his concern for the Saints there (section 97). Oliver Cowdery arrived in Kirtland three days later with some details about the horror the Saints were experiencing, details that would grow over time. Joseph worried. He was immersed in his own chaos in Kirtland and couldn't process what happened to the Saints in the place that was to be the center place of Zion (57:3). He needed instruction from the Lord. In a letter to Church leaders in Missouri shortly thereafter, we see him crying out, "O Lord What more dost thou require at their hands before thou wilt come and save them?"[2]

And the Lord was silent.

For four months.

Surely, the need for guidance from the Lord felt critical in this moment of despair—all the more urgent because it involved his fellow Saints, those who had chosen to follow him. However, Joseph had to wait.

In this instance, returning to the August revelation (97) might have helped him. We might read the revelation quickly and write off the beginning as a flowery preamble, yet when we consider Joseph's context, we begin to feel the weight of the words. Maybe those words didn't initially stick with Joseph, but they spoke directly to his current moment whether he recognized it or not. The revelation began with a reminder to Joseph that he and the Lord were friends. Joseph did not treat the value of friendship lightly—he would later call it "the grand fundamental prin[c]iple."[3] And he had developed his own relationship with the Lord over years, through many revelatory conversations. The Lord called His friend to "fear not," and to let his heart "be comforted." To rejoice, to be grateful, and to wait "patiently on the Lord." The Lord assured Joseph that He had heard him and that He had covenanted with Joseph "with an immutable covenant" that He would respond to his prayers. I want to pause here. We've discussed speaking as a part of God's character, but here, the covenantal language suggests that it isn't just God's inclination to speak and communicate with us, but it is a contract as we develop a relationship with Him. The timing might not be what we desire, but He will speak.

The Lord continued by assuring Joseph of the transformative power of His atonement, that "all things wherewith you have been afflicted shall work together for your good, and to my name's glory" (98:1–3). Things felt desperate, but Joseph had to continue to wait "patiently on the Lord." He had to lean into the silence if it were to transform him. Moreover, as the revelation continued, practicing patience would not only be necessary in communicating with the Lord but also in figuring out how to respond to the Saints' enemies patiently and not out of revenge (98:23).

By the middle of December, Joseph understood more completely the dire situation of the Saints in Jackson County. After four long months, the Lord spoke through him specifically to the Saints who had "been afflicted, and persecuted, and cast out." The Lord again testified of the importance of a relationship with Him and the transformational power of the atonement. He called out the Saints' sin. Yet He also offered reassurance that this tragedy, even with the Saints' own sins and failings, could be turned for their good. They were still His, and this pressure and darkness could transform them into His "jewels" (101:2–3).

Again, Joseph's task was to wait and trust in the Lord. "Let your hearts be comforted concerning Zion; for all flesh is in my hands; be still and know that I am God" (101:16). When I encounter a crisis in my own life, my first inclination is to put my head down and get to work—I feel like I just need to do something. However, the Lord doesn't often give me a laundry list of things to do or fix, but more often quietly whispers, "Be still." "Be still and know that I am God" is its own kind of action (Psalm 46:10, Doctrine and Covenants 101:16). And sometimes the most difficult thing the Lord asks of us. That was true in the 1833 crisis: The

Lord assured Joseph and the Jackson County Saints that in a future "day when the Lord shall come, he shall reveal all things," but for now, their charge was to be still (101:32).

Joseph's waiting did not paralyze him. He did what he could for the Saints in Jackson County with the information and the direction he already had. And sometimes, as we wait and lean into the darkness, we find our own answer by doing the opposite—the principle of indirection. This is best exemplified by one of the hard sayings of Jesus: "Whosoever will save his life shall lose it; and whosoever will lose his life for my sake shall find it" (Matthew 16:25). The only way to ultimately find our life is to do the opposite.

The Blessing of Mourning

At times in our lives, we will all experience loss, and at such times God's silence may feel most acute. Here, it may be helpful to think about the relationship between Alma's description of the part of our covenant to "mourn with those who mourn" (Mosiah 18:9) and God's desire to expand our relationship as He gives us light and understanding. Seasons of mourning, rather unexpectedly, can be seasons of abundant revelation.

Consider the function of mourning in Joseph's life. The tragic death of Joseph's oldest brother, Alvin, deeply affected him and his family. Alvin had not been baptized and at his funeral, the minister "intimated very strongly that he had gone to hell, for Alvin was not a Church member." Joseph Smith, Sr. "did not like it," nor did any of the family.[4]

Joseph's own mourning led him to seek the truth. An 1836 vision of Alvin in the celestial kingdom inspired Joseph to seek how all might receive salvific covenants (134). Later, mourning with others likewise set in motion revelation of other important truths. Mourning for a fellow Saint, at Seymour Brunson's funeral, Joseph taught the doctrine of baptism for the dead.[5] Mourning with Zina Huntington at the death of her mother led Joseph to teach of the Heavenly Mother of us all.[6] And Joseph used an opportunity to eulogize his friend King Follett to reinforce truths of our divine heritage and our potential to become like God.[7] Some of Joseph's most profound revelations came in the aftermath of grief and crisis. Living the part of our baptismal covenants to comfort and mourn and bear one another's burdens further sensitizes us to the Spirit and might open the way for revelation. Even those times when the heavens remain silent for the answer, getting outside ourselves can produce different light and understanding.

I don't venture to know exactly why silence comes, but I know it does. Yet, for what solace it might offer, we may know with surety that we are not alone. Perhaps this is one of the wintry doctrines of the gospel of which Elder Neal A. Maxwell taught: "There are in the gospel warm and cuddly doctrines, and then there are some that are just outright *wintry* doctrines.... One of them, frankly, is that we cannot approach [real] consecration without passing through [wintry] experiences, [because we don't achieve consecration] in the abstract."[8] Our mortal experience will not always be warm and cuddly—the Lord wants a "people tried in all things" (136:31). If Christ "descended below all things" (88:6), how can we feel entitled to a consistently bright path clear of obstacles to tread through mortality?

A dear friend of mine went through a period of deep mourning—a period of silence and darkness—when her father unexpectedly died. Two years earlier she had suddenly lost her younger sister and now her grief swelled. Her scriptures, where she had always gone for comfort to hear the Lord speak to her, became a raw and painful reminder of her father because they had always connected through their love of scripture. What had succeeded in bringing her peace before these tragedies no longer worked. Sometimes she felt paralyzed and the pain was excruciating. Her prior foundation was critical to her well-being. Though the absence and the silence she felt could not be fixed instantaneously, over time with considerable help from God, family, friends, and professionals she was able to return to her life. But she was changed. Elder Hugh B. Brown used to say, "Sometimes you walk in the light, sometimes you walk in the memory of the light."[9] Sometimes all we can do is hold on, but that relationship we already have with God will not be lost, despite the silence. Relationship endures.

The Irony of a Name

When Joseph called out from "the screeking iron do[o] rs, of a lonesome dark durty prison" they called Liberty,[10] the Lord didn't instantly relieve the pain and the worries. Rather, God taught Joseph "that all these things shall give thee experience, and shall be for thy good" (122:7). The Lord again pointed to the transformative power of His atonement as He had with the Jackson County expulsion. All the bad we experience, even if it is of our own making, can be transformed into something good because of Christ's atonement. Joseph's ironically named prison became a temple for what he learned. It was transformed into a sacred and holy place. And a significant part of what he learned was from the divine silence.

After nearly six months in the "durty prison," Joseph wrote a long letter to the Saints. He was nearing the end of this trial, but he didn't know that yet. Orson Pratt later prepared excerpts of Joseph's March 20, 1839, letter to "the Saints scattered abroad" for addition into the canon as sections 121–123. Orson abridged the document and offered us a collapsed view of Joseph's experience. While there are benefits to considering the revelation as canonized, to see how the revelation functioned in Joseph's own saintly narrative, we need more. If we consider Joseph's experience as recounted in his original letter, the divine silence for him becomes increasingly complex and far more widespread. He didn't ponder the silence for a few moments—a mere seven verses—only to immediately hear God's miraculous voice clearly speak peace to his soul (121:1–7).

In Joseph's complete letter, the paragraphs before the Lord spoke peace to Joseph begin to reveal the depth of the darkness he experienced and disabuse any notion of the potential immediacy of relief. In fact, the darkness and the silence began weeks earlier, when he described to Emma that "the contemplations, of the mind under these circumstances, defies the pen, or tongue, or Angels, to discribe, or paint, to the human being, who never experiance what we experience."[11] Yet, in this time of divine silence, the words of other holy ones, his friends, the Saints, sat on his heart and opened the way for him to hear the voice of God. He wrote of their letters, "all breathing a kind and consoling spirit ... they were to our souls as the gentle air is refreshing." These letters from his community offered him relief even as they simultaneously deepened his sadness at hearing of the Saints' extreme suffering. Moreover, the letters initiated a change to his own state. He said reading them seized "the presant with a vivasity of lightning it grasps after the future with the fearsness [fierceness] of a tiger it rhetrogrades from one thing to an other untill finally all enmity malice and hatred and past diferances misunderstandings and mismanagements lie slain victoms at the feet of hope." The silence began to fade when confronting the hope of his friends. He continued, "When the hart is sufficiently contrite then the voice of inspiration steals along and whispers my son pease be unto thy soul thine advirsity and thy afflictions shall be but a small moment."[12] It took time, support from friends, and his own contrition for the "voice of inspiration" to be able to "steal along" and whisper the Lord's word of peace to Joseph. Once it came, he still had to strain to hear the whisper.[13] His experience of the silence and the darkness ultimately enabled him to hear the voice of the Lord.

It is a striking thing to be writing a book on revelation

when you are experiencing your own period of silence in the heavens. I should say the heavens have not been completely silent, but in one specific area of my life I can hear a far-off pin drop. I mourn this silence and its accompanying privation, but somehow in the midst of the silence I have felt overwhelming gratitude for relationships and blessings. The silence has, unexpectedly, further solidified my own witness that God is there and God is a god who speaks. My friends—mortal and divine—stand by me. Sometimes absence understandably monopolizes our focus. Yet, absence can heighten our ability to better recognize presence, if we let it.

Elder Holland testified, "When you have to, you can have sacred, revelatory, profoundly instructive experiences with the Lord in *any* situation you are in. Indeed let me say that even a little stronger: You can have sacred, revelatory, profoundly instructive experience with the Lord *in the most miserable experiences of your life*—in the worst settings, while enduring the most painful injustices, when facing the insurmountable odds and opposition you have ever faced."[14] Like Joseph, we all need to learn by experience, and sometimes that experience includes divine silence. And we all need friends.

Coda

My Word Shall Not Pass Away

In mortality, we will always be limited. Our view and understanding of eternity will be frustratingly short most of the time. In the spring of 1831, with a number of curious manifestations of the Spirit in Kirtland, the Lord had these words for Joseph and the Saints:

> Behold, ye are little children and ye cannot bear all things now; ye must grow in grace and in the knowledge of the truth. Fear not, little children, for you are mine, and I have overcome the world, and you are of them that my Father hath given me; And none of them that my Father hath given me shall be lost. (50:40–42)

And then again, the following spring, just a couple weeks before another supremely lonely night of Joseph's life when he and Sidney were mobbed in Hiram, Ohio, the Lord had similar words of counsel for him:

> Verily, verily, I say unto you, ye are little children, and ye have not as yet understood how great blessings the Father hath in his own hands and prepared for you; And ye cannot bear all things now; nevertheless, be of good cheer, for I will lead you along. The kingdom is yours and the blessings thereof are yours, and the riches of eternity are yours. (78:17–18)

The Lord called to them and similarly calls out to us, His "little children." We could consider it infantilizing, but might I suggest that we regard it as a mark of our mortal limitations, our inability to "bear all things now," and our difficulty in understanding "how great blessings the Father hath ... prepared for" us? Rather than disparaging ourselves and our lack of capacity, we can focus on our title of being children of God, which testifies to our divine relationship. We are the literal children of God, and the Father has great blessings prepared for us. That relationship is a mark of our potential and our possibility. Moreover, because we have entered the covenant, we are also the children of Christ. The Lord uses the title of children to emphasize the opportunity we have in mortality to "grow in grace and in the knowledge of the truth" in a covenant relationship (50:40).

If we are His, we need not take counsel from our fears because Christ has "overcome the world." Christ never just tells us to plaster on a happy face to pretend everything is all right, but we can "be of good cheer'" because of Him. No matter our immediate circumstances, no matter what darkness and silence might lie ahead, He promises that "I will lead you along. The kingdom is yours and the blessings

IMAGE 4. Children playing on Provo road (ca. 1885), by George Edward Anderson. Image courtesy of L. Tom Perry Special Collections, Harold B. Lee Library, Brigham Young University.

thereof are yours, and the riches of eternity are yours" (78:17–18).

The Lord will lead us along. Sometimes, we will ever so slightly feel His hand nudging us, or maybe we will only recognize it long after the fact. Sometimes, the answer will come in a way we don't expect. Martha Cragun Cox was a mother of eight who had to bury three of her children. She was a curious, independent, loyal, itinerant teacher who brought education to children in small towns from southern Utah to northern Mexico. At one point in her life, when she was feeling desperately worried and weighed down with many things, she sought guidance and direction from God. It did not come in a way she expected. She wrote,

> I had a dream given me that gave me to see the condition into which I was falling. I thought I stood with a chain around my neck. This chain reached to the ground and was heavy with many bundles that were fastened to it, so heavy that I could not raise my head to look upward. Someone said to me, "If you must look at these all the time put them on this rod over your fire place and don't hang them on a chain about your neck or you will never see the sun and stars, and you should look up towards the heavens and not down." I then began to examine the parcels one by one and hang them on the rod.... All these while they seemed so heavy while hanging on my neck had no weight at all as I hung them on the rod.... That [last] bundle faded out through my fingers as I took it off the chain and lo, the chain was gone and I was free. When I awoke I resolved I would be free.[1]

There are times when what we need is to let go. Our burdens and the questions that weigh us down can be transformed through Christ's grace. These moments can build our relationship with God as we faithfully ask, wrestle, serve, and wait patiently. Ultimately, the Lord is the one who can free us from our burdens as He did with Martha and transform the questions and loads we carry into miraculous receptacles of divine light.

Joseph became one who walked and talked with God—but even he had to receive "revelation upon revelation, knowledge upon knowledge" and wait patiently on the Lord (42:61). The Lord is wholly trustworthy. As we humble ourselves and seek to build that faithful relationship, the Lord blesses us with deeper levels of trust, even amidst silence. That mortal weakness that we sometimes loathe is the very thing that leads us to ultimately become strong, to become like our heavenly parents. While we have the privilege of revelation in abundance, being in relationship with God is more important than seeing everything that lies ahead. Whatever the medium through which it comes, when God speaks—it is sure. The Lord speaks yesterday and today, "Though the heavens and the earth pass away, my word shall not pass away" (1:38).

Endnotes

Series Introduction

1. Ezra Taft Benson, "The Book of Mormon and the Doctrine and Covenants," *Ensign*, April 1987.

2. Minute Book 1 / "Conference A," 1832–1837. CHL. Also available at josephsmithpapers.org.

3. Jeffrey R. Holland, "The Maxwell Legacy in the 21st Century," *Neal A. Maxwell Institute for Religious Scholarship 2019 Annual Report*, 17.

4. Joseph Smith, "To the Elders of the Church of the Latter Day Saints," *Messenger and Advocate* 2.3 (December 1835), 229.

5. The "Prophecy of Enoch" in 1.3 (August 1832) lent weight to the Restoration project of Zion-building and described Enoch's encounter with a weeping God. The subsequent publication of additions to Genesis taught of a gospel known to Eve and Adam (1.10, March 1833, and 1.11, April 1833).

6. Joseph Smith quoted this definition from the *Theological Dictionary* of Charles Buck, on page 9 of the first printing of the Doctrine and Covenants.

7. Historical Introduction to Official Declaration 2, Doctrine and Covenants.

8. See *Joseph Smith's Uncanonized Revelations*, ed. Stephen O. Smoot and Brian C. Passatino (Provo, UT: Religious Studies Center, 2024).

Introduction. Revelation in Abundance

1. "Discourse by John Taylor," *Deseret News*, March 4, 1874, 68.

2. Revelation, n., *Oxford English Dictionary*.

3. Title page, Doctrine and Covenants.

4. Letter to the Church and Edward Partridge, March 20, 1839, 8, The Joseph Smith Papers, josephsmithpapers.org/paper-summary/letter-to-the-church-and-edward-partridge-20-march-1839/8 and Joseph Smith—History 1:17.

5. Rosemary Radford-Ruether, *Sexism and God-Talk: Toward a Feminist Theology*, 2nd ed. (Boston: Beacon Press, 1993).

6. Francine Bennion, "A Latter-day Saint Theology of Suffering," in *At the Pulpit: 185 Years of Discourses by Latter-day Saint Women*, ed. Jennifer Reeder and Kate Holbrook (Salt Lake City: Church Historians Press, 2017), 217.

7. "Briefly Moroni," Maxwell Institute Podcast with David Holland and Spencer Fluhman, November 17, 2020, #122.

8. Doctrine and Covenants 8:3, emphasis mine.

9. Joseph Smith to William W. Phelps, November 27, 1832, "Letterbook 1," 4, The Joseph Smith Papers, josephsmithpapers.org/paper-summary/letterbook-1/16.

10. Russell M. Nelson, "Revelation for the Church, Revelation for Our Lives," *Ensign*, May 2018.

1. The Voice of the Lord and Joseph Smith

1. Revelation, Hiram Township, OH, 1 Nov. 1831. Featured version, titled "77 Revelation Given in Hiram Nov. 1st. 1831," copied (between November 12 and 20, 1831), The Joseph Smith Papers, josephsmithpapers.org/paper-summary/revelation-1-november-1831-b-dc-1/1#source-note.

2. Doctrine and Covenants 1:2, 11, 24, 34, 38; and some of the examples in the revelations that follow: 6:2, 11:2, 12:2, 14:2, 35:8, 49:5, 63:6, 101:16.

3. Doctrine and Covenants 1:1; hearken, v. *Oxford English Dictionary*.

4. Scholars have dated the Tower experience over a decade-long period: 1508–9, 1511, 1512, 1513, 1514, 1515, or 1518–9. Euan Cameron, *The European Reformation* (Oxford: Clarendon Press, 1991), 171–174.

5. Martin Luther, *Martin Luther's Table Talk*, ed. Henry F. French (Minneapolis, MN: Fortress Press, 2017), entries: "Between June 9 and July 21, 1532," 101 and "September 12, 1538," 146.

6. Euan Cameron, *The European Reformation* (Oxford: Clarendon Press, 1991), 171–174.

7. Thomas Muntzer, "The Prague Protest," in *Revelation and Revolution: Basic Writings of Thomas Muntzer*, trans. and ed. Michael G. Baylor (Bethlehem, PA: Lehigh University Press, 1993), 55.

8. History, circa Summer 1832, 2, The Joseph Smith Papers, josephsmithpapers.org/paper-summary/history-circa-summer-1832/2.

9. Orson Pratt, *A Interesting Account of Several Remarkable Visions, and of the Late Discovery of Ancient American Records* (Edinburgh, Scotland: Ballantyne and Hughes, 1840). The copy used for transcription is held at CHL.

10. Terryl Givens, *By the Hand of Mormon* (New York: Oxford University Press, 2002), 219.

11. Avery Dulles, *Models of Revelation* (Dublin: Gill and Macmillan, 1983), 19.

12. Dulles, *Models of Revelation*, 27–28.

13. Givens, *By the Hand of Mormon*, 208–239.

14. Givens, *By the Hand of Mormon*, 219.

15. Catherine Brekus, *Strangers and Pilgrims: Female Preaching in America, 1740–1845* (Chapel Hill, NC: University of North Carolina Press, 1998), 32.

16. Jonathan Edwards, *The Works of Jonathan Edwards*, vol. 18, ed. Ava Chamberlain (New Haven: Yale University Press, 2000), 89–90.

17. Kingsley appeared before Edwards in a church council. Catherine Brekus, *Strangers and Pilgrims: Female Preaching in America, 1740–1845* (Chapel Hill, NC: University of North Carolina Press, 1998), 24.

18. Brekus, *Strangers and Pilgrims*, 98.

19. David Holland, *Sacred Borders: Continuing Revelation and Canonical Restraint* (New York: Oxford University Press, 2011).

20. Richard L. Bushman, "A Joseph Smith for the Twenty-First Century," in *Believing History: Latter-day Saint Essays* (New York: Columbia University Press, 2004), 274.

21. Jeffrey R. Holland, "Prophets, Seers, and Revelators," *Ensign*, November 2004, 8.

22. One of my research assistants, Andrew Jones, and I considered categorization and tallied all of the revelations. Classification, of course, is a subjective process, and others may do the work of classification a little differently. Andrew and Lindsey Meza have remarkable thoughtful minds, and their work as research assistants was invaluable to this book.

23. "Introduction to the Manuscript Revelation Books: Volume 1," The Joseph Smith Papers, josephsmithpapers.org/intro/introduction- to-revelations-and-translations-volume-1.

24. Joseph doesn't specify if he had the parchment in his possession or if he saw it in vision. In the years after it was received it was alternately understood as a "revelation" or as a "translation." For the purposes of my discussion, both a specific revelation and a translation fit under the larger umbrella of revelation. Book of Commandments, 1833, 18, The Joseph Smith Papers, josephsmithpapers.org/paper-summary/book-of-commandments-1833/22; and David W. Grua and William V. Smith, "The Tarrying of the Beloved Disciple: The Textual Foundation of the Account of John," in *Producing Ancient Scripture: Joseph's Smith's Translation Projects in the Development of Mormon Christianity*, ed. Michael H. MacKay, Mark Ashurst-McGee, and Brian M. Hauglid (Salt Lake City: University of Utah Press, 2020), 231–261.

25. Jeffrey R. Holland, "Prophets, Seers, and Revelators," *Ensign*, November 2004, 8.

2. Hearkening and Asking

1. Joseph Smith in Alexander Neibaur's Journal, May 24, 1844; February 5, 1841–April 16, 1862, 23–24; Church History Library, Salt Lake City, Utah, hereafter CHL.

2. Oliver Cowdery, "Letter IV," *Messenger and Advocate*, February 1835, 78. Emphasis mine.

3. History, circa Summer 1832, 2, The Joseph Smith Papers, josephsmithpapers.org/paper-summary/history-circa-summer-1832/2.

4. "Will," v., *Webster's 1828 Dictionary*, webstersdictionary1828.com/Dictionary/Will.

5. "Will," v. *Oxford English Dictionary*, oed.com/dictionary/will.

6. Russell M. Nelson, "Hear Him," *Ensign*, May 2020, 90.

7. Neal A. Maxwell, "According to the Desire of Our Hearts," *Ensign*, November 1996, 22.

8. Doctrine and Covenants 1:26; 6:7; 11:7, 21, 23; 88:63, 118; 97:1; 101:38; 106:3; 109:7; and some of asking: 4:7; 6:5–6; 7:1; 8:1, 9–11; 11:5; 12:5; 14:5; 14:8; 27:18; 29:6, 33; 35:9; 42:3, 56, 61, 62....

9. Elinor, her mother, and her siblings were racially categorized as "mulatto" in census records in the east, but Elinor was classified as white in Utah and California census records and likely avoided Latter-day Saint temple restrictions placed on women of African descent because she passed as white. E. G. Jones, "The Power of Prayer," in *At the Pulpit: 185 Years of Discourses by Latter-day Saint Women*, ed. Jennifer Reeder and Kate Holbrook (Salt Lake City: Church Historians Press, 2017), 75–78.

10. Dieter F. Uchtdorf, "The Reflection in the Water," CES Fireside, November 1, 2009.

11. Stephen E. Robinson and Dean Garrett, *A Commentary on the Doctrine and Covenants* (Salt Lake City: Deseret Book, 2001), 2:496.

12. Emma Anderson Liljenquist, "The Story of My Life," ca. 1948, 14–18; typescript; International Society Daughters of Utah Pioneers, Salt Lake City, in *The First Fifty Years of Relief Society*, ed. Jill Derr, et al. (Salt Lake City: Church Historian's Press, 2016), 533–534. In the nineteenth century, Latter-day Saint women often blessed others according to their faith as have believers since the time of Christ. See "Joseph Smith's Teachings about Priesthood, Temple, and Women," *Gospel Topics Essays*, churchofjesuschrist.org/study/manual/gospeltopics-essays/joseph-smiths-teachings-about-priesthood-temple-and-women?

13. Russell M. Nelson, "Sweet Power of Prayer," *Ensign*, May 2003.

14. Orson F. Whitney, "Newel K. Whitney," *Contributor* 6 (January 1885): 126.

15. Spencer Fluhman, "The University and the Kingdom of God," BYU Devotional, July 30, 2019, speeches.byu.edu/talks/j-spencer-fluhman/the-university-and-the-kingdom-of-god/.

16. Patrick Kearon, "God's Intent Is to Bring You Home," *Liahona*, May 2024, churchofjesuschrist.org/study/general-conference/2024/04/45kearon?

3. Scripture Abounds

1. See Janiece Johnson, "Becoming a People of the Book: Toward an Understanding of Early Mormon Converts and the New Word of the Lord," *Journal of Book of Mormon Studies* 27 (2018): 1–43.

2. Introduction, Book of Mormon, 1830.

3. William W. Phelps, "Letter No. 6," February 24, 1835, *Latter-day Saints Messenger and Advocate* (Kirtland, Ohio) 1/7 (April 1835): 97; "Annual Conference," *Deseret News*, April 11, 1860: 45, 48.

4. *Oxford English Dictionary*, canon, n.

5. Joseph Smith III, "Last Testimony of Sister Emma," *The Saints' Herald* 26:19 (October 1, 1879): 289.

6. Oliver Cowdery, Letter I, *Messenger and Advocate*, 1 (October 1834): 14.

7. William W. Phelps, *The Evening and the Morning Star, Prospectus, Evening and Morning Star*, June 1832 (January 1835), 1–2.

8. Revelation, April 1829–A (D&C 6), 14, The Joseph Smith Papers, josephsmithpapers.org/paper-summary/revelation-april-1829-a-dc-6/1#historical-intro.

9. *Oxford English Dictionary*, quick, adj. n., & adv.

10. *Oxford English Dictionary*, sharp, adj. n., & adv.

11. Elizabeth Haven, in *The Israel Barlow Story and Mormon Mores* (Salt Lake City: Ora H. Barlow, 1968), 139–41.

12. Elizabeth Haven Barlow to Elizabeth H. Bullard, February 24, 1839, Barlow Family Collection, CHL.

13. D. Todd Christofferson, "When Thou Art Converted," *Ensign*, May 2004, 11.

14. Quincy Newell, *Your Sister in the Gospel: The Life of Jane Manning James* (New York: Oxford University Press, 2019); Jane James, "'Aunt' Jane James" in "Joseph Smith, the Prophet," *Young Woman's Journal* 16: 551–552; Newell, "Afflicting the Comfortable: Jane James, American Racism, and The Church of Jesus Christ of Latter-day Saints," Maxwell Institute Lecture, October 18, 2019.

15. Quincy Newell first pointed out the significance of Jane's choice in "Afflicting the Comfortable: Jane James, American Racism, and The Church of Jesus Christ of Latter-day Saints," Maxwell Institute Lecture, October 18, 2019.

16. Editors of *Dialogue* [William G. Hartley], "Saint Without Priesthood: The Collected Testimonies of Ex-Slave Samuel D. Chambers," *Dialogue: A Journal of Mormon Thought*, vol. 12, no. 2 (1979): 13–21; Janiece Johnson and Quincy D. Newell, "'Not Only to the Gentiles, but Also to the African': Samuel Chambers and Scripture," *Church History*, vol. 92, no. 2 (June 2023): 357–381, doi.org/10.1017/S0009640723001439.

17. This is prior to the entry of boys into the deacon's quorum. The meticulous notes of British convert T. C. Jones document Samuel Chambers' witness and the influence of scripture on him.

18. Johnson and Newell, "'Not Only to the Gentiles,'" 366–381.

19. Johnson and Newell, "'Not Only to the Gentiles,'" 380.

20. John W. Wigger, *Taking Heaven by Storm: Methodism and the Rise of Popular Christianity in America* (New York: Oxford University Press, 1998), 29.

21. Bruce and Marie Hafen, "Crossing Thresholds and Becoming Equal Partners," *Ensign* (March 2007), site.churchofjesuschrist.org/study/ensign/2007/08/crossing-thresholds-and-becoming-equal-partners? Here they are paraphrasing Neal A. Maxwell, *Wherefore, Ye Must Press Forward* (Salt Lake City: Deseret Book, 1977), 127.

4. My Servant, Joseph Smith, Jr.

1. Orson F. Whitney, "Newel K. Whitney," *Contributor* 6 (January 1885): 126.

2. Newel Knight, History, private possession, copy in CHL.

3. Revelation, September 1830–B (D&C 28), 40, The Joseph Smith Papers, josephsmithpapers.org/paper-summary/revelation-september-1830-b-dc-28/1#source-note.

4. Dallin H. Oaks, "Two Lines of Communication," *Ensign*, November 2010, 83.

5. Dallin H. Oaks, "Two Lines of Communication," 86.

6. John Whitmer, History, 1831–circa 1847, 18, The Joseph Smith Papers, josephsmithpapers.org/paper-summary/john-whitmer-history-1831-circa-1847/22?p=22; Ardis Parshall, "In Kirtland, When the Mormons Were There," Keepapitchinin, keepapitchinin.org/2020/01/22/in-kirtland-when-the-mormons-were-there/.

7. Ezra Booth, "Letter II," *Painesville Telegraph*, December 20, 1831.

8. History, 1838–1856, volume B-1 (September 1, 1834–November 2, 1838), 795–6, The Joseph Smith Papers, josephsmithpapers.org/paper-summary/history-1838-1856-volume-b-1-1-september-1834-2-november-1838/250.

9. History, 1838–1856, volume B-1 (September 1, 1834–November 2, 1838), 796, The Joseph Smith Papers, josephsmithpapers.org/paper-summary/history-1838-1856-volume-b-1-1-september-1834-2-november-1838/250.

10. Mary A. Noble, "A Journal of Mary A. Noble," in Joseph Bates Noble Reminiscences, 1836–1866, CHL, 15, 76–78.

11. Lorenzo Snow in Eliza R. Snow, comp., *Biography and Family Record of Lorenzo Snow* (Salt Lake City: Deseret News Company, 1884), 13.

12. Desdemona Wadsworth Fullmer, Reminiscence, 1868, Desdemona Wadsworth Fullmer Papers, CHL, *The Witness of Women*, in Janiece Johnson and Jennifer Reeder (Salt Lake City: Deseret Book, 2016), 148.

13. Brigham Young, *Complete Discourses of Brigham Young* (Salt Lake City: The Smith-Petit Foundation, 2009), 4:1941.

14. Harold B. Lee, "Uphold the Hands of the President of the Church," *Ensign*, November 1970, 152, 153.

5. The Tyranny of a Burning Bosom

1. Richard G. Scott, "To Acquire Spiritual Guidance," *Ensign*, November 2009, 6–7.

2. Dallin H. Oaks, "Teaching and Learning by the Spirit," *Ensign*, March 1997, 13.

3. Richard J. Maynes, "The Joy of Living a Christ-Centered Life," *Ensign*, November 2015.

4. James Faust, "Did You Get the Right Message?" *Ensign*, April 2004.

5. James Faust, "Did You Get the Right Message?"

6. Karen Lynn Davidson and Jill Mulvay Derr, *Eliza: The Life and Faith of Eliza R. Snow* (Salt Lake City: Deseret Book, 2013), 12–15.

7. Alan Taylor, "Rediscovering the Context of Joseph Smith's Treasure Seeking," *Dialogue: A Journal of Mormon Thought* 19:4 (1986), 19. See also Alan Taylor, "The Early Republic's Supernatural Economy:

Treasure Seeking in the American Northeast, 1780–1830," *American Quarterly* 38:1 (Spring 1986): 6–34.

6. Growing into the Principle of Revelation

1. Joseph Smith Discourse, between circa June 26 and circa July 2, 1839, as reported by Willard Richards, 21–22, The Joseph Smith Papers, josephsmithpapers.org/paper-summary/discourse-between-circa-26-june-and-circa-2-july-1839-as-reported-by-willard-richards/7 and as reported by Wilford Woodruff, 34–5, The Joseph Smith Papers, josephsmithpapers.org/paper-summary/discourse-between-circa-26-june-and-circa-2-july-1839-as-reported-by-wilford-woodruff/9.

2. Julie Beck, "And upon the Handmaids in Those Days Will I Pour Out My Spirit," *Ensign*, May 2010, churchofjesuschrist.org/study/general-conference/2010/04/and-upon-the-handmaids-in-those-days-will-i-pour-out-my-spirit?

3. Joseph Smith Discourse as reported by Wilford Woodruff, 34–5.

4. Russell M. Nelson, "Grow into the Spirit of Revelation," *Liahona*, January 2021, churchofjesuschrist.org/study/liahona/2021/01/grow-into-the-principle-of-revelation.

5. Joseph Smith Discourse as reported by Wilford Woodruff, 34–5.

6. Henry David Thoreau, *The Essential Thoreau* (New York: Simon and Schuster, 2013), 419.

7. Neal A. Maxwell, "Apply the Atoning Blood of Christ," *Ensign*, November 1997.

8. Doctrine and Covenants 18:10, 10:17, 8:5, 42:30.

9. Revelation, April 1829–B (D&C 8), 13, The Joseph Smith Papers, josephsmithpapers.org/paper-summary/revelation-april-1829-b-dc-8/2.

10. Steven Harper, *Making Sense of the Doctrine and Covenants* (Salt Lake City: Deseret Book, 2008), 43.

11. Jeffrey R. Holland, "Cast Not Away Therefore Your Confidence," BYU Devotional, March 2, 1999, speeches.byu.edu/talks/jeffrey-r-holland/cast-not-away-therefore-your-confidence/.

12. Jeffrey R. Holland, "Cast Not Away Therefore Your Confidence."

13. Jeffrey R. Holland, "Cast Not Away Therefore Your Confidence."

14. Mary Fielding to Mercy Fielding Thompson, August–September 1837, Mary Fielding Smith Collection, CHL.

15. Mary Fielding to Mercy Fielding Thompson, August–September 1837, Mary Fielding Smith Collection, CHL.

16. Russell M. Nelson, "Let God Prevail," *Ensign*, November 2020, 93.

7. Cautionary Tales

1. Doctrine and Covenants 45:57, 46:8, 90:5.

2. Journal, 1835–1836, 23, The Joseph Smith Papers, josephsmithpapers.org/paper-summary/journal-1835-1836/23-24.

3. Parley P. Pratt, *The Autobiography of Parley Parker Pratt* (New York: Russell Brothers, 1874), 65.

4. Pratt, *The Autobiography of Parley Parker Pratt*, 65; Revelation, 9 May 1831 (D&C 50), 82, The Joseph Smith Papers, josephsmithpapers.org/paper-summary/revelation-9-may-1831-dc-50/1#historical-intro.

5. Russell M. Nelson, "Revelation for the Church, Revelation for Our Lives," *Ensign*, May 2018.

6. Revelation, May 9, 1831 (D&C 50), 82, The Joseph Smith Papers, josephsmithpapers.org/paper-summary/revelation-9-may-1831-dc-50/1#historical-intro.

7. Dale G. Renlund, "Observation, Reason, Faith, and Revelation," BYU Devotional, August 22, 2023.

8. M. Russell Ballard, "Women of Dedication, Faith, Determination, and Action," BYU Women's Conference, May 1, 2015.

9. M. Russell Ballard, "Women of Dedication, Faith, Determination, and Action."

10. Karen Lynn Davidson, "Each Life that Touches Ours for Good," *Hymns*, 1985, no. 293.

11. Jane Smith Coleman, "Words of Encouragement," *Woman's Exponent* 2, no. 16 (January 15, 1874), 127; Janiece Johnson and Jennifer Reeder, *Witness of Women: Firsthand Experiences and Testimonies from the Restoration* (Salt Lake City: Deseret Book, 2016), 47–48.

12. William E. Berrett, as quoted by Dallin H. Oaks, "Teaching and Learning by the Spirit," *Ensign*, March 1977.

13. Dallin H. Oaks, "Timing," BYU Devotional, January 29, 2002.

14. Neal A. Maxwell, "Hope through the Atonement of Jesus Christ," *Ensign*, November 1998.

15. Neal A. Maxwell, "Plow in Hope," *Ensign*, May 2001.

16. Henry B. Eyring, "Education for Real Life," *Ensign*, October 2002.

17. Dieter F. Uchtdorf, "Acting on the Truths of the Gospel of Jesus Christ," Worldwide Leadership Training, January 2012.

8. When Silence Reigns

1. Adam Miller, *Letters to a Young Mormon*, 2nd ed. (Salt Lake City: Deseret Book, 2018), 35–36.

2. Letter to Church Leaders in Jackson County, Missouri, August 18, 1833, 1, The Joseph Smith Papers, josephsmithpapers.org/paper-summary/letter-to-church-leaders-in-jackson-county-missouri-18-august-1833.

3. Journal, December 1842–June 1844; Book 3, July 15, 1843–February 29, 1844, 13, The Joseph Smith Papers, josephsmithpapers.org/paper-summary/journal-december-1842-june-1844-book-3-15-july-1843-29-february-1844/19?highlight=friendship%20the%20grand%20fundamental.

4. William Smith, *Deseret News*, January 20, 1894.

5. Simon Baker, "15 Aug. 1840 Minutes of Recollection of Joseph Smith's Sermon," Joseph Smith Collection, CHL.

6. Susa Young Gates, *History of the Young Ladies' Mutual Improvement Association of the Church of Jesus Christ of Latter-Day Saints* (Salt Lake City: Deseret News, 1911), 15–16.

7. "Accounts of the 'King Follett Sermon,'" The Joseph Smith Papers, josephsmithpapers.org/site/accounts-of-the-king-follett-sermon.

8. Bruce C. Hafen, *A Disciple's Life: The Biography of Neal A. Maxwell* (Salt Lake City: Deseret Book, 2002), 20.

9. Sam Brown, Twitter, 8/25/22, twitter.com/sambrown_lds/status/1562767483869663232.

10. Letter to Emma Smith, April 4, 1839, 1, The Joseph Smith Papers, josephsmithpapers.org/paper-summary/letter-to-emma-smith-4-april-1839/1.

11. Letter to Emma Smith, April 4, 1839, 1, The Joseph Smith Papers, josephsmithpapers.org/paper-summary/letter-to-emma-smith-4-april-1839/1.

12. Letter to the Church and Edward Partridge, March 20, 1839, 8, The Joseph Smith Papers, josephsmithpapers.org/paper-summary/letter-to-the-church-and-edward-partridge-20-march-1839/8.

13. Letter to the Church and Edward Partridge, March 20, 1839.

14. Jeffrey R. Holland, "The Lessons of Liberty Jail," CES Fireside, September 7, 2008.

Coda. My Word Shall Not Pass Away

1. Martha Cragun Cox, "Biographical Record of Martha Cragun Cox: Written for My Children and my Children's Children, and All Who May Care to Read it," CHL.

Scripture Index

Doctrine and Covenants
D&C 1:1 13, 25, 130
D&C 1:2 13
D&C 1:2, 11, 24, 34, 38 130
D&C 1:4 42, 59, 95
D&C 1:4, 17 58
D&C 1:6 13
D&C 1:9–16 58
D&C 1:11 14, 29
D&C 1:17 12, 26, 59, 60
D&C 1:20 18, 26, 55, 61
D&C 1:24 71, 72
D&C 1:26 133
D&C 1:24–28 84
D&C 1:29 22
D&C 1:34 14
D&C 1:37 vii
D&C 1:38 127
D&C 3:3 87
D&C 3:7 87
D&C 3:10 88
D&C 4:1 43
D&C 4:7 133
D&C 6:1 43
D&C 6:2 44, 130
D&C 6:5 86
D&C 6:5–6 133
D&C 6:6 89
D&C 6:7 133
D&C 6:11 32
D&C 6:14 86

D&C 6:22 86
D&C 6:23 87
D&C 7:1 133
D&C 7:9 87
D&C 8:1, 10 86
D&C 8:1, 9–11 133
D&C 8:2 90
D&C 8:3 91, 130
D&C 8:6 88
D&C 9 71
D&C 9:7 86
D&C 9:8 69, 73
D&C 11:1 43
D&C 11:2 44, 130
D&C 11:5 133
D&C 11:7, 21, 23 133
D&C 11:21 45
D&C 12:1 43
D&C 12:2 44, 130
D&C 12:5 133
D&C 14:1 43
D&C 14:2 44, 130
D&C 14:5 133
D&C 14:8 133
D&C 15:4 30
D&C 16:4 30, 39
D&C 20 5
D&C 20:5 28
D&C 20:8 60
D&C 20:9–11 41
D&C 20:11 41

D&C 20:42, 46, 59 53
D&C 20:77 9
D&C 20–21 60
D&C 21:1 60
D&C 21:5 60
D&C 25:7 54
D&C 25:7, 16 ix
D&C 25:16 54
D&C 26:1 45
D&C 26:2 55
D&C 27:2 106
D&C 27:18 133
D&C 28 6
D&C 28:2 61, 62
D&C 28:5 62
D&C 28:7 62
D&C 28:11 62
D&C 28:13 55, 63
D&C 29:6, 33 133
D&C 29:7 14, 45
D&C 29:34 104
D&C 29:35 106
D&C 33:16 45
D&C 35:8 130
D&C 35:9 133
D&C 35:20 45
D&C 38:12 111
D&C 38:32 7
D&C 39:10 9
D&C 42 98
D&C 42:3, 56, 61, 62 133
D&C 42:56 43
D&C 42:61 127
D&C 43 6
D&C 43:2 64
D&C 43:3 65
D&C 45:57 138
D&C 46–52 99
D&C 46:1 33
D&C 46:2 34
D&C 46:3 33
D&C 46:5–6 33
D&C 46:7 28, 34, 35, 96
D&C 46:8 36, 138
D&C 46:9 36
D&C 47:4 43

D&C 49:2 109
D&C 49:5 130
D&C 50:2 95, 96
D&C 50:2–5 99
D&C 50:8 99
D&C 50:10–11 99
D&C 50:17 100
D&C 50:17–25 100
D&C 50:22 100
D&C 50:40 124
D&C 50:40–42 123
D&C 50:41–46 101
D&C 51:3 104
D&C 52:15–16 101
D&C 52:17 101
D&C 52:33 101
D&C 54:2, 8 107
D&C 57:3 113
D&C 58:26–28 108
D&C 58:44 30
D&C 60:2, 5 107
D&C 61:21–22 107
D&C 62:5 107
D&C 63:6 130
D&C 64:31–33 108
D&C 64:34 vii
D&C 70:3 43
D&C 70:13–14 104
D&C 72:8 37
D&C 76 5, 46
D&C 76:15–20 47
D&C 76:28, 49 47
D&C 76:95 105
D&C 76:115–117 47
D&C 76:118 47
D&C 78:5–6 105
D&C 78:17–18 124, 126
D&C 84:43–44 46
D&C 84:57 46
D&C 88:6 118
D&C 88:62–63 112
D&C 88:63 ix
D&C 88:63, 118 133
D&C 88:95 111
D&C 90:5 138
D&C 95:16 30

D&C 97 113, 114
D&C 97:1 133
D&C 98 6
D&C 98:1–3 115
D&C 98:2 26, 109
D&C 98:12 84
D&C 98:23 115
D&C 101 6
D&C 101:2–3 115
D&C 101:16 115, 130
D&C 101:32 116
D&C 101:38 133
D&C 106:3 133
D&C 109:7 133
D&C 112:4 53
D&C 121 6
D&C 121:1–2 111
D&C 121:1–7 119
D&C 121:3, 7 111
D&C 121:26 77
D&C 122:7 119
D&C 128:21 84
D&C 130:4–7 108
D&C 134 117
D&C 136:31 118
D&C 138 5
D&C 138:1–6 48
D&C 138:11 48

Old Testament
Exodus 4:10, 14 89
Exodus 14:10–12 91
Exodus 14:13 91
Exodus 14:16 92
Psalm 46:10 115
Psalm 83:1 112
Isaiah 28:10 84
Isaiah 51:9 59
Isaiah 55:6–8 112
Joel 2:28 81

New Testament
Matthew 7:7–9 61
Matthew 13:51–53 ix
Matthew 16:25 116
Mark 4:36–41 59
Luke 5:1–7 60
John 5:29 46
1 Corinthians 13:9–10, 12 8
2 Corinthians 3:3 35
2 Corinthians 3:6 110
1 Peter 3:18–20 48
Hebrews 4:12 44
James 1:5 16, 28

Book of Mormon
1 Nephi 22:9 53
2 Nephi 3:17 7
2 Nephi 8:9–11 59
2 Nephi 28:30 84
Jacob 4:13 8
Mosiah 18:9 116
Alma 32:27 29
Mormon 9:32 22
Moroni 4:3 9
Moroni 10:4 28

Pearl of Great Price
JSH 1:15–16 97
JSH 1:16 97
JSH 1:17 130
JSH 1:21 97
JSH 1:25 16
Article of Faith 9 1